Prenups for Lovers

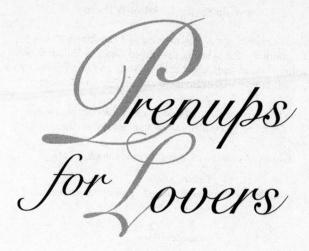

Prenups for Lovers

A Romantic Guide
to Prenuptial
Agreements

Arlene G. Dubin

VILLARD · NEW YORK

Library of Congress Cataloging-in-Publication Data

Dubin, Arlene G.
Prenups for lovers: a romantic guide to prenuptial agreements / Arlene G. Dubin.
p.   cm.
Includes index.
ISBN 0-375-75535-7
1. Antenuptial contracts—United States—Popular works.
2. Marriage counseling—Popular works. I. Title.
KF529.Z9 D83 2001
346.7301'6—dc21
00-043370

Random House website address: www.atrandom.com

Printed in the United States of America on acid-free paper

24689753

First Edition

Text design by Meryl Sussman Levavi/Digitext

This book is dedicated to
Mom and Dad
Susan and Bud
The Four Corners of My World

PLEASE NOTE

This book is intended to present the case in favor of prenuptial agreements and provide a broad, general overview. It is *not* a substitute for separate and independent counsel for you and your partner. The laws in this area are complex. They vary from state to state and change periodically. You should consult with an experienced attorney to apply the relevant law in your state to your unique situation.

All names, occupations, and other identifying details of any real-life scenarios in this book have been changed to protect the privacy of the individuals involved. Any resemblances to real persons are purely coincidental and unintentional.

CONTENTS

✥

Part Three

DO IT YOUR WAY:
SPECIAL SITUATIONS 155

Prenups for Lovers

MOONLIGHT, ROSES, AND
PRENUPS

&

After a twelve-year marriage and a seven-year divorce proceeding, I married a lifelong bachelor. How did we do it? Although the complete answer could be the subject of another book, a principal reason is our prenuptial agreement.

Since my prenup paved the way to a magical marriage, it obviously has a great deal of sentimental value to me. I have it placed in a Tiffany bowl in our living room along with my dried bouquet and other romantic reminders of our wedding.

The reason that our prenup catapulted our relationship into marriage is because it enabled us, admittedly each a bit marriage challenged, to confront our worst fears. Concerned that I might become a two-time loser in marriage, I didn't want to lose another seven years in a divorce proceeding. As for my husband, in the event that bachelorhood *was* his ultimate destiny, he wanted to avoid any unpleasant property disputes.

Perhaps the greatest value of our prenup, though, was in its successful negotiation to completion. The process promoted honesty and openness and strengthened the bond between us. There is an old bromide that money is the last thing that people talk about before marriage and the first thing they fight about after marriage. That didn't happen to us! We had avoided our first fight.

We disclosed our assets and liabilities, expressed ourselves as to how these would be handled in various possible scenarios, and—what do you know?—we were still wild about each other. In fact, we felt closer than ever, because these practical, mundane issues were no longer ticking time bombs. Our relationship was grounded in reality, not illusion; we were marrying for *love,* not money. Our prenup swept aside the business part of our relationship, allowing us to enjoy the pleasures of our anticipated union.

From the vantage point of my own situation as well as my matrimonial practice, I have seen a prenup as a marriage *enabler* and a marriage *enhancer.* I have concluded that a prenup is for just about everyone. It should be standard issue for impending nuptials, along with the license and the ring, and part of the romance of courtship, like moonlight and roses.

A CRASH COURSE IN FAMILY LAW

Flashback to my divorce: Over the course of seven years, my ex-husband and I each were represented by serial lawyers. (Unfortunately, this is the norm in matrimonial cases, although Patricia Duff in her tiff with Revlon billionaire Ronald Perelman may have abused the privilege with her twenty-five teams of lawyers.)

During this protracted proceeding, I took a crash course in family law. My case introduced me to the gamut of family law issues—equitable distribution, pension split-ups, divorce taxes, child support and custody, etc. I knew I could do legal work as well as or better than the next lawyer, so I researched, studied, and investigated and emerged an expert in the field.

For my entire legal career of more than twenty years, I have had the privilege of practicing law with my partners at RubinBaum LLP in New York City. Our firm represents corporations, entrepreneurial enterprises, and individuals in a full-service general practice. At the time of my divorce, I specialized in employee benefits and executive compensation. Our firm had done prenuptial agreements, but generally referred matrimonial work to other lawyers. After my divorce, I convinced my partners to turn matrimonial work over to me. I had the education, the experience, and, most important, the empathy.

HOW I LEARNED TO LOVE PRENUPS AND HOW YOU WILL TOO!

In the course of practicing domestic relations law, I became passionate about prenups.

One of my observations is the transmogrifying effect of divorce on the human personality; it brings out a hidden dark side in many people. Your beloved becomes bedeviled. Your kitten becomes a wildcat.

In this negatively charged atmosphere, individuals are supposed to make rational choices profoundly affecting the rest of their lives. Most mortals cannot accomplish this feat. Many of us resort to counterproductive litigation rather than compromise and conciliation. We go out of our way—*far* out of our way—to disrupt the process and dismay the soon-to-be ex. As the late criminal defense lawyer Louis Nizer once said, "There is no murder trial, nothing that happens in the law, as acrimonious as divorce."

A prenup is a vaccine against this virulent illness. You discuss your concerns openly in advance and negotiate solutions when you are favorably disposed to your intended and in an atmosphere of mutual good faith. You arrive at a fair solution without the need for expensive and lengthy litigation. You spend less time extricating yourself from a failed relationship and more time ushering in your new life. And your children suffer far fewer side effects. A prenup assures that, in the off chance that you do end up in divorce court, you will be treated on an outpatient basis—*not* in the intensive care unit.

PRENUPS PRECEDE HAPPY MARRIAGES

By entering into a prenup, you decrease your divorce odds in the first place—simply by its process. At the outset of your lives together, you establish a framework for problem solving that will form a solid and secure basis for a mature and thriving marriage.

A prenup functions as a catalyst to communication because it requires a critical examination of sensitive issues, such as children and money, and a resolution that's acceptable to both of you. You become conversant in compromise. In addition, a prenup precipitates openness since it requires full financial disclosure. Talking about money is tough, but once you've opened this door, it leads to communication in other areas. Thus, you establish a precedent for dialogue, enhancing the prospects for a happy marriage.

Further, a prenup fosters education. When you apply for a marriage license in a particular state, you agree to be bound by the domestic relations and trusts and estates laws of that state. But what does that mean? Do you know what the law provides? There is no driver's manual with a summary of the applicable laws, and no road test to demonstrate mastery of them.

If you are planning to marry, you owe it to yourself to engage in this educational exercise, and this book can help you. For example, if the marriage goes awry, do you know how much support you may owe your spouse? Do you know that your spouse may be entitled to a portion of your property *even* if the property is in your name only? Do you know that your spouse may have a stake in your 401(k) plan, your inheritance, or the value of your business? Do you know that your spouse *automatically* may be entitled to a portion of your estate? You should know the answers to these questions *before* you walk down the aisle.

ONE SIZE DOESN'T FIT ALL

Divorce law takes a one-size-fits-all approach, whereas a prenup is your opportunity to tailor the law to your preferences. In a prenuptial agreement, you *customize* the arrangements of your marriage. You make your own deal.

As a prospective bride or groom, you generally don't agree with all the state-mandated rules and don't feel that they make sense in the context of your own situation. Alternatively, you don't always feel comfortable with the uncertainty and unpredictability of modern matrimonial law. The prenuptial agreement generally permits you to make your own rules and clarify, modify, or flatly reject the laws that are not right for you.

Like it or not, marriage is in part a contract. It's more romantic to create your own than to accept the form that has been prefabricated by the government.

PRENUPS BECOME PREVALENT

Although prenuptial agreements were used in ancient Egypt, going back five thousand years, they have become common currency in the United States only in the last two decades. In twenty years the number of prenups has quintupled. Today, they are making, breaking, and shaping the emotional and financial contours of relationships between men and women in ever-growing numbers.

So what *is* a prenuptial agreement? Very simply, it is a private agreement between a couple contemplating marriage. The couple arranges, in advance, financial matters in the event of death or divorce and may opt to include "lifestyle" or nonfinancial topics.

Sometimes called premarital or antenuptial agreements, prenups in the United States used to be the playthings of the rich and famous. But as people become more and more aware of the value of prenups, they are increasingly commonplace in the landscape of middle-class America.

A prenup is a very effective and flexible document with wide-ranging applications. A prenup may insulate you or your partner from each other's student or business loans, credit card debt, and support obligations. It may differentiate premarital and post-marital property. It may protect property acquired by gift or inheritance. It may specify in advance the amount or percentage of alimony, child support, and/or equitable distribution payable in the event of divorce. It may provide a method to value problematical items such as stock options, pension plans, professional degrees, and business interests. And/or it may set forth the amount or percentage of a death benefit.

EVEN MARRIED PEOPLE DO IT

In addition to engaged couples, married people are also writing agreements these days. Some married couples might want to amend their prenups; some who do not have prenuptial agreements might want to enter into marital contracts or postnuptial agreements, or as I prefer to call them, internuptial agreements. (An internup is like a prenup, except it is entered into *during* marriage by a husband and wife.) Increasingly today people are not marrying; these same-sex or nonmarried couples are consummating cohabitation agreements or, as I call them, quasi-nups.

TAKE THE WORRY OUT OF MARRIAGE

I believe that mystery is good in novels and movies, but not in marriage. To enter a prospective lifetime partnership in an atmosphere of confidence and trust, you and your partner must freely exchange ideas and information. In this way you maximize your chances for a successful union.

The fear of divorce and its unknown consequences are major factors deterring marriage. A prenup removes the uncertainty because it clearly states your rights and obligations at the outset in the event the worst-case scenario occurs. In other words, a prenup encourages and promotes marriage.

If a condom takes the worry out of sex, then a prenup takes the worry out of marriage.

Prenups Are for Lovers

I am writing this primer on prenups to help you *understand* these agreements and show you how to make optimum use of yours. In part 1, I tell you *why* you need a prenup and, in part 2, *how* to go about obtaining one. In part 3, I counsel you on certain *special situations* that arise, for example, if you are young, mature, a parent, a business owner, married, or living together. I also show how prenups *help,* rather than hurt, women.

This is a why-to-do-it and how-to-do-it book, but not a do-it-yourself book. The law of premarital contracting varies somewhat from state to state, although subject to the same general overall principles. To comply with these laws and ensure that your prenup will hold up, you and your partner each should consult with an attorney. By reading this book, you will learn how to work effectively and efficiently with your attorney to craft an appropriate agreement.

Despite the overwhelming advantages of prenups

and their greater prevalence, they are still somewhat misunderstood and so sometimes maligned. I've heard reactions such as: "I could never do that to *her.*" "I wouldn't cheat him/her like that." "I wouldn't marry him if I didn't trust him." "It's cold." "It's heartless." "It's *unromantic.*"

To counteract the negative image created by the term "prenuptial agreement" or "prenup," maybe a semantic change is in order. Perhaps we should refer to the arrangement as "PNA," an acronym for Pre-Nuptial Agreement. Because of its similarity to "DNA," it sounds like a life-giving force.

My mission in this book is to debunk the prenup myths and spread my message that prenups are for lovers. They can enhance communication, improve the quality of your marriage, and heighten its emotional and intellectual dimension. They can reduce the incidence of divorce and reduce bitter aftereffects if there is a divorce.

I wish you all a prenup as a prelude to a romantic marriage, and I hope that you and your partner keep it among your souvenirs and never use it unless death does you part.

Part One

Before I'd Say

"I Do,"

I'd Do a Prenup

Why to Do It

Chapter 1

WHY YOU NEED
A PRENUP

&

A BOUQUET OF
TWO DOZEN REASONS

tatistics are scarce in the prenuptial area. Anecdotal evidence suggests that at most about 20 percent of couples now enter into prenups. By 2020, I predict that more than 50 percent of couples will be preceded down the aisle by prenups. Here are two dozen reasons why:

1. YOU'RE LIVING IN THE REAL WORLD. Since 1960, as a result of no-fault divorces and societal acceptance, the divorce rate in the United States has doubled. Currently the divorce rate is about four to five out of every ten marriages. The median duration for a first marriage that ends in divorce is 6.3 years and is even shorter for a remarriage.

You probably believe you have the right stuff to beat these grim statistics, but studies show that almost all people getting married are sure divorce won't happen to *them*. Further, prenups dictate the disposition of assets upon death. You do believe that will ultimately happen to you, *don't you?*

2. DIVORCE LAWS ARE A-CHANGING. Forty-one states and the District of Columbia rely on "equitable distribution," which provides a court with broad discretion to split the value of assets. Even in the remaining "community property" states, a court exercises some subjective judgment. In a prenup, you and your partner can clarify and write the rules of your marriage. Otherwise, you may leave yourself at the mercy of a total stranger—an arbitrarily assigned judge—to decide your fate.

3. YOU'RE WORTH MORE THAN YOU THINK. You're marrying later these days—the median age is 25 for a woman and 26.8 for a man—and by the time you do, you've begun to accumulate assets (as well as acumen). You may think you don't have savings—but your 401(k) plan is savings. What about your stock options? life insurance policy? a prospective inheritance? your home or your car?

The number of millionaires jumped from 1.9 million to 8 million from 1989 to 1999. Even if you're not a millennial millionaire, you probably benefited in some way from the stock market, IPO, Internet, and 401(k) boom since the 1990s. You'll want to hold on to your nest egg, no matter how small or large it is.

4. YOUR PARENTS ARE WORTH MORE THAN YOU THINK. This country's greatest intergenerational transfer of wealth in history—from the "Depression" generation to

the "baby boomer" generation and their "boomlet" off-spring—is occurring over the next few decades. In the next half-century, at least $40 trillion will be handed down. Your prenup will ensure that your parents' hard-earned heirlooms (and cash) all stay in the family.

5. THE "LITTLE WOMAN" GROWS UP. Women have entered the job market, risen through the ranks, even broken the glass ceiling, and they want to protect the progress they've made. At the same time, women in traditional roles have become more assertive about the value of nonmonetary contributions to marriage.

6. YOU'RE LIVING TO A RIPE OLD AGE. At the beginning of the twentieth century, the estimated life expectancy was 46.3 for a male and 48.3 for a female. By the end of the twentieth century, life spans increased to 79.1 for women and 73.1 for men. As medicine advances, longevity will increase, further increasing the chances that you will be married more than once.

7. YOU'RE ON THE REMARRIAGE MARRY-GO-ROUND. Rising divorce rates have led to rising remarriage rates: 75 percent of divorced people remarry within five years. Further ratcheting up the remarriage rate is longevity. Since the failure rate for second and subsequent marriages is even higher than for first marriages—a whopping 60 percent—you need a prenup more than ever.

8. TAKE CARE OF YOUR CHILDREN AND DEPENDENTS. In a prenup, you can arrange for the payment of support and tuition for your children from a prior marriage. You can provide your children with an appropriate inheritance. You also can take care of aging parents or a disabled relative.

9. SAVE THE FAMILY JEWELS. Since your spouse most likely would be entitled to a share of your family or small business in the event of a divorce, you need a prenup to prevent potentially disruptive litigation. Equally important, you and your family members or business partners must protect yourselves against the transfer of a business to an ex-spouse or liquidation of the business to pay off the ex-spouse.

10. DON'T FALL ON YOUR ASSETS. Your prenup enables you to protect valuables, such as your pension plan, your vacation hideaway, your season tickets to the Denver Broncos, and your rent-controlled apartment, as well as your newly minted MBA or J.D. or unsold software program or screenplay or novel. You need to protect not only the current value of your assets, but also their future limitless worth.

11. CHERISH THE MEMORIES. In your prenup, you can make sure that your family's cabin, artwork, jewelry, antiques, and anything of sentimental value stays in the family.

12. STAY OUT OF DEBT (NOT ONLY YOURS BUT YOUR PARTNER'S!). Prenups point out and protect you from your beloved's indebtedness, whether student loan, gambling, business, or credit card debts.

13. GET YOUR JUST DESSERT. A prenup can ensure you are justly compensated, for example, if you suspend a career to relocate, raise a family, or support your spouse in a professional or trade school.

14. STRENGTHEN THE BOND BETWEEN YOU. You share information and discuss sensitive matters. You express op-

timism that you will be able to raise and resolve press-
ing problems. You create a mechanism for further dialogue and dispute resolution.

15. TRUMP THE TRICK. By full disclosure, you and your
partner put your financial cards on the table up front,
thus playing with a full deck on financial matters. Since
studies show that monetary issues are responsible for
70 percent of divorces, you're both way ahead of the
game.

16. PLAY GOVERNOR! You veto laws that you don't like
or that are inappropriate for your situation. For example, the law in your state may automatically entitle your
spouse to one-third of your estate. But you may want to
leave your estate to your children from a prior marriage.
Or you may desire to leave your entire estate to your
partner—but that's the point: *You* should make the
choice. You can override this legal mandate by entering
into a prenup.

17. STAY OUT OF MURKY LEGAL WATERS. In many states,
"separate" property *is not* split up in a divorce and includes premarital property and gifts and inheritances
acquired after marriage. By contrast, "marital" or "community" property *is* split up in divorce and generally
consists of earnings from employment after marriage.
Despite the seemingly clear distinction between these
types of property, the line easily can become blurred. In
a prenup, you can define separate and marital property
the way you see fit.

18. REDUCE LEGAL FEES. The cost of a prenup is a bargain compared to the cost of contentious divorce or probate proceedings. The average price of a wedding party

is $20,000. For a fraction of that amount, you can make a lasting investment in a prenup.

19. AVOID "DIVORCE, INCORPORATED," as *New York* magazine calls the cabal of divorce lawyers who control the divorce "system" in New York City. They charge a lot, they're clubby, and they may have their own agenda. You can circumvent any such clique in your hometown if you have a prenup.

20. BE SELF-RELIANT. A prenup reminds you that your marriage license is not a meal ticket and that ultimately each of you must rely upon yourself to make your way in this world. It prevents you from being lulled into a false sense of security about the financial ever-after of marriage and discourages you from unduly leaning on your partner. It encourages you to be independent, which in turn gives you the strength and resources to cope with the economic vicissitudes of life, irrespective of your marital status.

21. ALLEVIATE ANXIETY. With a prenup, you minimize the chance for adversarial proceedings, reducing the amount of vengeance and improving the outlook for the next stage of your life and the healthy development of your children. You needn't stay stuck in a bad marriage. You needn't dread the legal process of ending your marriage.

22. GOT TO GET A "GET"? Prenups are custom-made documents providing for specialized, even religious, needs. In a prenup a man may agree to grant a "get"—a Jewish divorce—in the event of civil divorce. In another specialized situation, you may use a form of premarital

contract to adopt a system of "covenant" marriage which, in states like Arizona and Louisiana, makes it more difficult to divorce.

23. BE A GOOD CITIZEN. By opting for a prenup, you don't waste the resources of the courtroom in the adjudication of essentially private domestic matters.

24. CONTROL YOUR OWN DESTINY. You don't default to the state system. You and your partner write a marriage contract to suit your individual needs. In the words of the poet William Ernest Henley in the poem "Invictus," "I am the master of my fate, I am the captain of my soul."

Chapter 2

DEBUNKING THE
PRENUP MYTHS

❦

*L*ike sexual myths, the misconceptions surrounding prenups could fill a *Bulfinch's Mythology.* Misinformation and lack of information have given prenups a bad name. A prenup is often seen as cold and calculating, cynical and sinister, even as a prescription for divorce. My advice: Don't prejudge a prenup.

I'd like to stand the prenup myths on their Hydraheads. The following reality check shows that a prenup is an important step you can take to improve your relationship with your partner and increase your chances of experiencing happily ever after.

Let's debunk some myths:

MYTH 1. A PRENUP JINXES THE MARRIAGE.

Reality: This is tantamount to saying that if you write a will, you will die sooner; if you take out fire insurance on your home, your house is more likely to burn down; or if you buy long-term care insurance, you are more likely to end up in a nursing home.

You might view your prenup as a form of catastrophe insurance or divorce insurance without annual premiums. If you consider the high incidence of divorce in the general population, a prenup seems like an exceptionally good preventative measure.

Discussion of the possibility of divorce and the eventuality of death should strengthen your relationship, make you aware of its fragility, and give you heightened respect for your union.

MYTH 2. THE BETTER-OFF PARTY TAKES ADVANTAGE OF THE LESS-WELL-OFF PARTY IN A PRENUP. IT'S NOT FAIR!

Reality: In order for a prenup to be upheld, it must reflect fundamental fairness. Harsh terms that leave one spouse woefully undersupported could be successfully challenged. A lopsided agreement will simply not pass muster.

During the engagement, you and your partner are in love. You are negotiating in an optimistic atmosphere of mutual goodwill. It is therefore likely that you will be more reasonable and generous toward each other than during a divorce, when you may feel disappointed, hostile, or vengeful.

It is in both of your best interests to make a fair deal. If you are the less-well-off party, you will improve your financial position. If you are the better-off party, you will have an agreement that is likely to stand up in court. Plus both of you will have the peace of mind that your marriage is off to a good start.

MYTH 3. PRENUPS ARE BAD FOR WOMEN.

Reality: Prenups can empower women. You can use a prenup to ensure that nonmonetary contributions—such as being a career wife—will be valued. A prenup can provide that you will receive proper compensation if you make a career sacrifice—for example, if you give up your career to raise children, you work part-time, or you lose your job because you relocate for your spouse. You can use it to clarify your financial arrangements in advance, rather than gamble in court, where you will be subject to an unknown judge's biases and value systems.

MYTH 4. A PRENUP REDUCES MARRIAGE TO A COLD BUSINESS DEAL.

Reality: When you get married, whether you realize it or not, you agree to be bound by the family and probate laws of your state. These laws generally view marriage as an economic partnership (now that's a cold business deal). A prenup provides you with the opportunity to familiarize yourselves with these laws, decide whether these laws make sense for you, and in fact, to override them, if you conclude that you don't want these laws to apply to your relationship. You have the chance to customize the laws. A prenup is far more personal than the alternative.

PRENUPS ARE NO NEW AGE FAD

We may think of a prenup as a newfangled device for modern marrieds in the new millennium; the truth is they've been around for about five millennia. Historical evidence exists that parties entered into premarital contracts going all the way back to Ancient Egypt.

Recently, scientists have been able to use a high-tech ionizing blower to restore ancient Egyptian documents discovered in 1899. These finds included papyrus documents that were used to wrap mummified crocodiles, which were considered sacred offerings to the gods. Among the papyrus documents that were found wrapped around the crocodiles were *prenuptial agreements!* (Perhaps that's why some divorcing couples behave like crocodiles trying to devour as much as they can sink their jaws into.)

Anthropologists and historians have also found examples of primitive prenups among the ancient Babylonians, Hebrews, and Muslims on through Anglo-Saxon society, the Middle Ages, and Elizabethan England.

Marriage contracts were commonplace in England up until Lord Hartwicke's Act of 1753, which eliminated common law marriage and required couples to be married in a church.

MYTH 5. A PRENUP MAKES IT
TOO EASY TO DIVORCE.

Reality: It is never easy to divorce, although a prenup makes the mechanics easier. On the other hand, a prenup strengthens the relationship in the first place, making it less likely that any unraveling will occur.

In the event of divorce, a prenup removes the financial issues from contention, thus reducing hostility and bitterness. It helps you to maintain cordial relations in a post-divorce relationship, which is particularly important if you are parents.

Today the conventional wisdom—from sociological, psychological, and legal standpoints—is that people should not stay together in "dead" marriages. A prenup eases the transition and enables both of you to move on with your lives.

MYTH 6. A PRENUP IS EXPENSIVE.

Reality: A prenup can range in price from $150 to tens of thousands of dollars. For every dollar spent on a prenup, it is estimated that from $10 to $1,000 is saved in legal fees in a divorce. A prenup may be one of the best investments you'll ever make.

MYTH 7. PRENUPS ARE ONLY FOR THE
GLAMORATI.

Reality: Prenups are not only for celebrities, tycoons, and moguls, but also for just about everyone. For example, prenups are critical if your parents are planning to make gifts or leave you an inheritance. They are essential if you own family businesses or professional licenses or practices. If you choose to support your partner through professional school or training, a prenup can ensure your fair share of the graduate's eventual income stream. A prenup may protect you against your spouse's creditors. Prenups are imperative if you have responsibilities to children from a previous marriage or to aging parents. Finally, prenups are necessary to cover special issues applicable to older people, such as estate planning, Social Security, Medicare/Medicaid, and long-term care.

MYTH 8. IF I BRING UP THE ISSUE OF A PRENUP, MY INTENDED WILL BE HURT, OFFENDED, AND INSULTED.

Reality: You may be surprised.

If you voice your desire to have a prenup in a fair, loving way, your partner shouldn't be offended or angry. More likely than not, your intended will be relieved to get his/her issues out in the open and clarify his/her responsibilities.

You should bring up the topic as early as possible in a serious relationship, explain in detail why you want one, and work it out in a collaborative way.

The biggest mistake you can make is not to raise the topic at all. Almost as bad is to be dogmatic about it.

And remember—if you can't talk about touchy topics, it doesn't bode well for a happy marriage.

MYTH 9. A PRENUP SAYS, "I DON'T LOVE YOU, I DON'T TRUST YOU."

Reality: A prenup says I love you and trust you so much that I can share even my most intimate secrets. It is well known that people are intensely private about their money. Most would sooner talk about their sex lives. But in a prenup, you are candid with your partner about money matters. You disclose the full extent of your assets and your debts. You don't hold back.

In a prenup you initiate a dialogue that leads you to nonfinancial or lifestyle matters, such as careers and work schedules and the sharing of household and child-rearing responsibilities. You express your innermost dreams, hopes, demons, and doubts.

You love and trust your partner enough to tell the truth. You impart deep confidences and exchange sensitive information. You don't dodge the difficult issues. You have faith that whatever you reveal, your partner will accept, and whatever your differences, you and your partner will resolve them.

MYTH 10. MY INTENDED AND I KNOW EACH OTHER VERY WELL AND HAVE WORKED OUT OUR ISSUES VERBALLY. WE DON'T NEED IT IN WRITING.

Reality: As legendary Hollywood producer Samuel Goldwyn said many years ago, "A verbal agreement isn't worth the paper it's written on." You and your partner may have different recollections of what you agreed upon. You may have different understandings of how your agreement applies in different situations. With the passage of time, you may forget what compromises you made. You may not understand the implications of what you said. You may have overlooked certain critical issues or made unwarranted or erroneous assumptions. What's more, your agreement may not be enforceable because laws generally require premarital contracts to be in writing. In short, you need a written legal document to make sure your wishes are carried out.

"DON'T GET BURNED"

When Roseanne was asked why she didn't have a prenuptial agreement with former husband Tom Arnold, the comedienne snapped, "I was stupid. He got millions and millions—the pig." Both she and Arnold were recovering alcoholics, and to prove that she loved him, she agreed to marry without a prenup. With next husband, bodyguard Ben Thomas, she changed her tune: "Oh, honey, there'll be prenuptial agreements up the ying-yang," she said.

After three years of marriage, Roseanne filed to divorce Thomas. According to the couple's prenup, Roseanne agreed to pay her husband $250,000 annually for the first five years of marriage. Thomas also got $150,000 to buy a new home.

The fiery comic counseled, "Don't get burned." In other words, get your fire insurance in the form of a prenup.

MYTH 11. I DON'T NEED A PRENUP BECAUSE I PLAN TO LIVE WITH MY SIGNIFICANT OTHER, RATHER THAN MARRY HIM/HER.

Reality: If you cohabit with your significant other, you may want a cohabitation or living-together agreement.

A "cohab" determines how your assets will be distributed if your relationship ends.

If you and your partner live together in contemplation of a permanent relationship, you need a "cohab" arguably more than an engaged couple needs a prenup. Cohabitants, unlike married persons, don't have even state family or probate laws as safety nets. In general, you will be treated as two unrelated single persons in the event your relationship ends for any reason.

Although in some states cohabitants may gain some rights through theories of "implied-in-fact" contracts, such contracts are difficult and expensive to prove. Accordingly, you can't rely on such legalities to arrange your affairs.

MYTH 12. A PRENUP SAYS, "DON'T TOUCH MY MONEY."

Reality: The essence of a prenup is its flexibility. A prenup can say just about anything you choose, as long as it is not manifestly unfair and not illegal.

A prenup can say, What's yours is yours, and what's mine is mine. But it doesn't have to say that—and it often doesn't. For example, a prenup can say, What's yours is mine and vice versa. Or it can say, Whatever you acquire before marriage is yours, and whatever I acquire beforehand is mine, but we share whatever we acquire afterward. A prenup can distinguish among different types of property. Or a prenup can promise a specified amount or percentage of assets in the event of divorce or death. Or it can protect something (e.g., a family home) that's of particular emotional value.

MYTH 13. PRENUPS ARE NOT FOR YOUNG PEOPLE JUST STARTING OUT.

Reality: The opposite is true. Since young people typically don't have assets at the outset of the marriage, an entire pot of assets acquired after marriage is potentially in dispute—homes, retirement assets, stocks, bonds, and other property. Young people have possibilities. Today's waitress may be tomorrow's movie star, and today's computer geek may be tomorrow's e-mogul, and such prospects may be protected in a prenup.

Further, as a young person, you may wish to decide how to handle your debts or agree, in advance, to share your assets fifty-fifty, some other ratio, or not at all. You may need a prenup for a specific situation, for example, if you support your partner through graduate or professional school or put your education or career on hold to have children or if you forgo a job or a career in a relocation.

MYTH 14. A PRENUP IS UNNECESSARY BECAUSE OUR LEGAL SYSTEM TAKES CARE OF THESE MATTERS IN THE EVENT OF DIVORCE OR DEATH.

Reality: Although most states provide a mechanism for consensual divorce, most parties find it extremely difficult to agree to terms. Typically angry and hurt, they are governed by emotion rather than logic. Divorce lawyers are often unable to control the strong feelings of their clients and are sometimes even accused of fanning the flames.

If you go to court to resolve your differences, you expose yourself to a time-consuming, expensive, and emotionally draining process as well. You also subject yourself to the vagaries of the judicial system.

Judges have far-reaching discretion in matrimonial matters. They make decisions based on their subjective judgment and their own value systems, and these may or may not harmonize with yours. Your fate may depend on the advocacy of the attorneys and the impression the judge may have formed on the basis of such advocacy.

Do you want to take your chances with the legal system? Assuming your partner is not a complete lout (which is safe to assume; otherwise you wouldn't be marrying this person), you almost always do better to negotiate a prenup, even if it's imperfect.

MYTH 15. A PRENUP IS USELESS BECAUSE IT CAN'T POSSIBLY ANTICIPATE WHAT MAY HAPPEN IN A MARRIAGE.

Reality: Prenups are organic documents. You may include as many or as few issues in a prenup as you want. As your marriage matures, you may resolve additional issues or new issues that arise as a result of changed circumstances. You can amend, modify, or supplement a prenup by agreement after marriage.

An agreement between spouses that is entered into during marriage is called an internuptial agreement ("internup") or postnuptial agreement. An internup is distinguished from a separation agreement, which is entered into in contemplation of divorce. The binding effect of an internup is similar to that of a prenup. Both the prenup and the internup are undertaken with the expectation that the marriage will flourish.

Chapter 3

TAKING THE MYTH
OUT OF MARRIAGE

☙

THE PSYCHOLOGY OF PRENUPS

The Beast falls in love with Beauty. When Beauty kisses the Beast, the Beast turns into a handsome Prince. Beauty and the Prince prepare to wed. The Prince says to Beauty, "First, you must agree that if the marriage doesn't work out, the castle will stay with my family."

Would this be material for a Disney musical?

Probably not. The original story is illusionary entertainment. The above version destroys the fantasy and ruins the romance of everlasting love.

For this same reason, you may resist a prenup. For many people, marriage is a big-screen Technicolor movie, with a happy Hollywood ending.

You should overcome any resistance, though, and

here's why: Marriage is not a movie or a musical or a fairy tale.

You can enjoy the fantasy of a movie at the same time you know that the movie is not real. The knowledge of reality does not spoil the movie. With this same kind of duality, you can have your prenup and your romance, too. And a better marriage.

The preceding chapter covered the myriad myths of prenuptial agreements. This chapter deals with one monolithic myth—the myth of marriage. This chapter is about the ways that a prenuptial agreement—in the

---

DEAR ABBY ADVISES

In response to a letter from "Old-Fashioned Southern Lady," who resisted a prenup on the ground that it shouts, "I do not trust you," Abigail Van Buren wrote in her column:

Please rethink your position and do not regard his insistence on having a prenuptial agreement as an insult. The purpose is to protect BOTH parties should the unthinkable occur. . . . I have always urged couples contemplating marriage, particularly those who have been married before and have children, to have a prenuptial agreement. In the event of death or divorce, it can prevent grief, heartache, and misunderstanding. It brings to mind the Boy Scout motto, "Be Prepared."

course of demythologizing marriage—can enhance your wedded bliss.

Most of us marry with no small number of expectations, hopes, and dreams. You have a fantasy of who you are and who your companion is. Your upcoming marriage seems thrilling because it encompasses these wonderful unspoken fantasies.

The prenuptial agreement gives you an opportunity to articulate and share one another's dreams. What are your aspirations? What are your partner's? If this exchange sounds frightening to you, it shouldn't. The best chance you have of living up to one another's expectations is knowing what they are in advance and finding out what it is that your partner holds dear.

By virtue of this process, your prenup actually *protects* your romance. A relationship built on reality is stronger than a relationship built on illusion. The agreement thus provides a fertile ground upon which a beautiful marriage can blossom.

PRENUPS BUTTRESS RELATIONSHIPS

A prenup needn't upset the pleasure of your dreams. You can enjoy your fantasy at the same time that you face the possibility that it may not be realized. Further, your prenup can intensify the pleasure of your relationship—by drawing out your desires, promoting communication, and enabling you and your partner to establish the rules of your relationship. By telling each other what's important to you, you make it *more* likely that you will each get what you want.

"The prenuptial agreement doesn't threaten the splendor of the prospective liaison and can *buttress* the future relationship, rather than burden it," says Dr.

Samuel Abrams, psychiatrist and psychoanalyst, New York City. "A skillfully engaged prenuptial dialogue can serve to distinguish those expectations that can be realized from those that will put an unwelcome hardship on the attendant relationship."

PRENUPS ARTICULATE YOUR EXPECTATIONS

A leading cause of marital breakdown is unmet expectations.

The value of a prenup is that it clearly states what is otherwise an enduring presence in the marriage that you and your beloved probably are not aware of—each other's aspirations. For example, you may have an unspoken desire that your husband will take care of you financially forever. Or that your wife will attend to your every need: your home, your meals, your laundry, your children. In a prenup you discuss the parameters of your marriage and make sure that illusionary wishes do not unwittingly become part of the marriage by default.

As Dr. Abrams says: "Openly agreed upon rules are likely to be a better foundation for growth than are those latent rules that surface and prove to be either disagreeable or downright outrageous. ('What do you mean, you *don't* do dishes?')"

PRENUPS WED PRAGMATISM AND ROMANCE

In addition to providing a context to discuss each other's dreams, prenups enable you to work through differences that you may uncover when you talk about each other's expectations.

"The dialogue and agreement provide concrete counterpoints to being swept away by romance, hope, and illusion. Marriage without love is likely to be wooden, but marriage without regard to actualities is likely to be shaky. The prenuptial dialogue *weds* pragmatism with romance. The successful integration of the two is a far better foundation than any marked leaning one way or the other," says Dr. Abrams.

Denise Zalman, C. S. W., psychoanalyst and couple therapist, New York City, agrees: "One cannot just think about love when one gets married. But many people don't want to think about practical matters because it detracts from the fantasy that being in love is enough to get married. The prenuptial agreement helps focus people on practical matters."

Dr. Richard Shoup, psychotherapist, marriage and family counselor, New York City, feels that the romantic ideal that is built into Western culture may deter good relationships, because it can cloud your judgments and cause you to gloss over issues. "The ideal is detrimental to relationships because it masks the real work involved in relationships that is not always pleasant."

PRENUPS DEMYSTIFY MONEY

For most people, it's harder to talk about money than sex. Money matters raise more personal issues of self-worth and self-esteem than discussing sex. Some people in love feel it is vulgar to mention money—it's mixing the sacred and the profane.

But money is a real part of marriage—which is an economic *and* emotional partnership. You're probably spending money to get married and along with your love, finances will be an integral part of your relationship. All the love in the world cannot protect you from the fact that you'll have to pay bills and make countless everyday choices about spending money.

The prenup provides a setting for disclosing your current financial assets and liabilities and creating the ground rules for the future. It allows you to integrate the topic of money into your marriage in a way that will not threaten the romance—but coexist peacefully with it.

PRENUPS PREVIEW LIFESTYLE

Once you start talking about your assets and liabilities, it becomes easier to continue to talk about money and other personal issues. Since communication is the key to happy relationships, prenups can have an overall effect of reducing tension and promoting harmony.

You should talk openly about how you handle your finances, what you think is going to be your arrangement in terms of work, and particularly, if you are a woman and want to work and have children, how you'll balance these demands.

Dr. Don K. Smith, licensed marriage, family, and child counselor in Orange, California, comments on lifestyle agreements: "From a psychological standpoint, premarital agreements promote emotional bonding and attachment. They encourage openness and honesty and force couples to look at themselves and share with one another. They facilitate problem solving and foster growth and development."

Through a prenup, pesky money and lifestyle issues are resolved up front, freeing you to focus on each other's characteristics and attributes that sparked your romance in the first place.

PRENUPS PREPARE YOU FOR MARRIAGE

The Catholic Church has long recognized the value of prenuptial dialogue in a marital preparation process called PreCana. The couple meets with a pastoral team, who raise issues about family, sexuality, lifestyle issues, and, of course, finances.

According to Monsignor Edward Scharfenberger, judicial vicar in the diocese of Brooklyn, New York, "My personal view is that there are certain facts that people who are going to get married should know. Even if it's a turn-off, it's better that they find out before than after."

The biggest problems, says Msgr. Scharfenberger, arise when the couple has not discussed in advance financial and other issues. "The prenuptial agreement might serve the purpose of raising issues that people wouldn't think of. Maybe it would save trouble and heartache later."

This process itself can strengthen relationships. "A lot of people find that by sharing intimate and romantic details of their lives they feel closer to each other because they feel they know each other better. So sometimes I think that the truth can enhance romance," says Msgr. Scharfenberger.

PRENUPS RAISE YOUR CONSCIOUSNESS

Responding to the need for greater marriage preparation, several states now offer discounts on marriage li-

censes for couples who take premarital courses, and
some high schools include courses on marital skills in
their curricula.

A prenuptial agreement provides intensive and individual instruction. You confront issues, rather than
avoid them. You don't take the path of least resistance—
you act *consciously*.

It is possible that after considering a prenup, you
might decide ultimately not to enter into one. Nevertheless, you will have benefited by the knowledge and understanding that you gained, not only about your rights
and obligations under the law, but also about your partner's thoughts, values, and beliefs.

PRENUPS PROVIDE A LITMUS TEST

Dr. Shoup points out that prenups "can clear up some
potential problems that couples have down the road."

If a problem arises over the prenup, it is probably
symptomatic of a problem in the relationship. "I don't
think that couples break up over prenups. They break
up over other things. I think the ability to work out the
prenuptial agreement can be a litmus test of the relationship," adds Dr. Shoup.

Ms. Zalman puts it another way: "Just as money issues are rarely about money, the prenup often stands for
other issues in the relationship that can't be resolved.
What we need to do is go beyond the symbolic issues
and look at the actual issues."

Tips from Counselors

Professional counselors encourage people getting married to do the following, all of which occur in the process of negotiating a prenuptial agreement:

♥ Communicate, communicate, communicate.
♥ Have a dialogue about money, sex, children, parents, religion, and any and all sensitive topics.
♥ Be totally honest and open.
♥ Don't have unrealistic expectations.
♥ Face reality first, then indulge your fantasies.
♥ Be practical as well as romantic.
♥ Take care of your children from a previous marriage, aging parents, and disabled relatives.

Prenups, According to Dr. Ruth K. Westheimer ("Dr. Ruth")

Dr. Ruth K. Westheimer ("Dr. Ruth"), sex therapist and media personality, notes that a relationship that breaks up over a prenup likely would have foundered anyway. "Even if the topic is a little upsetting, a good relationship, based upon mutual love and the desire to make a life together, is not likely to break up because of that suggestion. If it does break up because of that issue, then you have to say, 'Boy, am I glad I did not marry that person because that was not meant to be.'"

A prenup allows you to build a better relationship because you have the difficult issues out of the way. Dr. Westheimer points out: "While getting over that initial psychological feeling of 'Oh, God, Why Doesn't He or She Trust Me?,' you could clear the air. It could help by saying, 'Okay, this is like a will or a living will. It is something that has to be done, it's done, now let's go on from here.' "

Dr. Westheimer says: "We live in such a litigious society. Nobody knows what life brings. Hopefully we will never need it. What's the big deal? Let's do it and give it to the attorneys. I would say don't have the prenuptial agreement tucked away under your pillow. That might interfere with your sex life. But put it in a safe or better yet in your attorney's file.

"For the new millennium, a prenup is part of a mature relationship, based on love, mutual trust, and optimism."

There is every indication that prenups will be common in the future. The more prenups become the norm, the easier it will be for you and your partner to discuss them in a matter-of-fact way. The more you know about each other, the more realistic your expectations, the more likely your marriage will succeed . . . and the more likely you will live happily ever after . . . just like in the movies!

Chapter 4

INDIVIDUAL PROFILES

g

NOT JUST FOR THE RICH AND FAMOUS, BUT FOR SOMEONE *REALLY* IMPORTANT—*YOU!*

*T*n this chapter, you will find yourself or someone who very closely resembles you or a family member
or someone you know. You or that close friend or relative needs a prenup.

A prenup is for anyone with any property at all—a
401(k) plan, an IRA, a home, jewelry, stock options, a stock
portfolio, mutual funds, or an expectation of receiving a
bonus, gift, or inheritance. Anyone with debts. Anyone
who is on track toward or has already obtained a degree,
certificate, or license or has launched or built a career,
business, or professional practice. Anyone who possesses
a creative product—a novel, a painting, a screenplay, a
software program, a patent or an invention—sold or unsold. Anyone with children from a prior relationship.

In short, prenups are for just about everyone:

- ♥ Young couples starting out
- ♥ Couples with family issues—businesses, gifts, and inheritances
- ♥ Mature couples in remarriages and mid-careers

YOUNG COUPLES STARTING OUT

CASE STUDY 1. STUDENT DEBTS

Patrick and Elaine are both in their early twenties. Patrick, who just graduated from college and is looking forward to a management internship position, owes $20,000 in student loans. Elaine is starting out as an actuary and expects to save some of her earnings. Elaine is head over heels in love with Patrick but in a tailspin about Patrick's educational debts.

In a prenuptial agreement, Patrick and Elaine agree that their respective earnings after marriage will be considered "separate" property and thus *not* subject to division in divorce. Elaine's savings will be kept in Elaine's name alone so that they will be unreachable by Patrick's creditors.

Patrick and Elaine also provide a "sunset" clause in their prenup—the prenup automatically expires when their marriage lasts for seven years (when the debt will be paid off).

The prenup provides Elaine with the security that in the event the marriage is short-lived, she will not lose her hard-earned savings to Patrick's creditors. It also focuses the couple's attention on Patrick's indebtedness and helps them to plan for repayment through proper

SON BRINGS SUNSET

Burt Reynolds's prenuptial agreement with Loni Anderson contained a "sunset" clause: If they had a child, the agreement automatically terminated. Since they adopted their son, Quinton, this provision was triggered.

In most states, you can provide in your prenup that it will "sunset" after the passage of a certain period of time without the need for any action on anyone's part. If divorce or death occurs after that time, your prenup has no force or effect. The ten-year anniversary is a common benchmark.

About 60 percent of all divorces occur in the first eight years. A sunset clause allows you to express the expectation of a permanent union at the same time that it guards against the consequences of a short-lived marriage. Thus, a sunset clause can be a fair compromise if one party wants a prenup and the other doesn't. Also, it can guarantee that you don't end up with a petrified prenup—that is, an antiquated agreement that has not been updated to consider changes in your circumstances.

budgeting. And through the inclusion of a sunset clause, they show their long-term commitment to each other.

CASE STUDY 2. SEPARATE ACCOUNTS

Corey is a sales manager for a manufacturing company and earns $60,000 a year, while Cynthia is a yoga instructor earning $18,000 a year. Both are under thirty, and neither has been married before. Corey has accumulated $50,000 through his investments in mutual funds.

Corey and Cynthia enter into a prenup in which they agree that Corey will keep his mutual funds in a separate account. Cynthia waives any right to such funds. They also agree that they will pool their earnings after the marriage and keep such property in joint names. In the event of divorce, they will divide such earnings equally.

The prenup thus protects the property that Corey brings into the marriage in the event of divorce. Although the rule in their particular state is that property brought into the marriage is considered "separate," the existence of such separate property must be proven. The prenup provides a concrete record of the valuation of the mutual funds at the time of the marriage. Especially with respect to stocks and other financial assets, such records may not be retained, and after-the-fact reconstruction tends to be next to impossible. In addition, the prenup clarifies that the appreciation on his separate property is likewise separate.

At the same time, the prenup states the couple's intention to divide *equally* all the fruits of both their labors during the marriage even though Corey earns substantially more than Cynthia.

CASE STUDY 3. STOCK OPTIONS

Regina, a human resources executive, has been granted stock options and anticipates additional grants. Her fiancé is Norman, a hospital administrator. Regina's options are not vested until she puts in a certain amount of time at the company. The options are 20 percent vested after one year, 40 percent after two years, 60 percent after three years, 80 percent after four years, and 100 percent after five years. In addition, they are exercisable for a certain period of time after they become vested.

When will Regina's stock options become "marital/community property" and subject to division if she and Norman divorced? Is it at the time of grant? The time the stock options become vested? How would the stock options be valued if the marriage terminates before they are exercised? The law is evolving in this area and may be difficult to apply.

Regina and Norman write a prenup to answer these questions for themselves. They state that the options granted before marriage would remain separate property. With regard to the options granted after marriage, they would become marital/community property at the time the options become vested. They agree that the stock options would be valued according to a widely-known pricing formula called "Black-Scholes." They also decide that Norman would be entitled to one-third of the value of such stock options.

Regina and Norman have answered questions in advance—thus staving off uncertainty and expensive litigation.

CASE STUDY 4. SUPPORT OF A STUDENT SPOUSE

Barbara, an office manager, plans to support Robert through law school. Robert has his sights on a law firm partnership. Since Robert will obtain both his law license and his law practice after the marriage, both will become part of the marital pot in their state. Both will need to be valued in order to be divided.

The valuation of a law license and law practice is not an exact science. Rather it is a highly subjective procedure, leading possibly to dramatically different conclusions by forensic accountants or business appraisers. Also, it requires "discovery," an onerous and intrusive process that requires considerable disclosure of financial information.

Barbara worries about the legendary workload of a young associate on a partner track—and the effect on their marriage. Since Barbara is making a sacrifice to enable Robert to reach his career goal, she is entitled to be compensated in the event of divorce. Thus, Robert promises to pay Barbara a graduated (and fair) amount based on average income and years of marriage—a so-called escalator or staircase arrangement. In exchange, Barbara waives all claims to Robert's law license and law practice, obviating the need for a valuation of such assets.

CASE STUDY 5. GIVING UP A CAREER

Diana teaches piano. She plans to marry Mark, an investment banker. Diana and Mark want to have children soon, and they agree that Diana will be a full-time mother and homemaker.

Diana believes that marriage is an economic partnership and that nonmonetary contributions are just as important as materialistic ones. Thus, Diana and Mark agree that in the event of divorce, they would divide their property fifty-fifty. Diana would remain in the marital residence until the youngest child is eighteen, with Mark paying the mortgage, real estate taxes, insur-

THE "ESCALATOR" CLAUSE

In 1996 John F. Kennedy Jr. and Carolyn Bessette signed a prenup with a sliding scale of compensation in the event of divorce. She was to get $1 million if the marriage broke up within the first three years of marriage, $2 million if the couple split after three to ten years, and $3 million after ten years of marriage. At the time, JFK Jr.'s fortune was estimated at $33 million. They had been married three years when they perished in the tragic airplane crash in the summer of 1999.

In their prenup, beloved John-John and his bride agreed to a so-called escalator or staircase clause. Such a clause addresses the commonly shared belief that as a marriage endures, the economic partnership grows and the payout on divorce or death should increase.

ance premium, and repairs. When the house is sold, they would divide the net proceeds in half. In addition, Diana and Mark agree on a maintenance amount and the duration for which Mark would be responsible.

In exchange, Diana waives her interest in Mark's MBA degree and career as an investment banker. Thus, Mark avoids a thorny issue of whether a degree or a career is intangible property to be valued and split upon divorce.

FAMILY BUSINESSES, GIFTS, AND
INHERITANCES

CASE STUDY 1. MOM-AND-POP BUSINESS

Nancy, who works in her parents' hardware store, in which she is a shareholder, and Michael, a computer technician, are engaged. Nancy's parents are worried about the business falling out of family hands. This might happen if Nancy were required to give Michael stock in the family business as a divorce settlement or death benefit. In addition, Nancy's parents dread the prospect of valuing the hardware business in the event of divorce or death.

To solve the problem, Michael signs a prenup in which he waives any interest in the family business.

Michael has written a software program which he believes will be a big seller. He also has accumulated substantial savings in his employer's 401(k) plan. The company invested its matching contributions in its own stock, which outpaced the S&P Index in the nineties bull market. In their prenup, as a quid pro quo, Nancy waives any rights she might have in Michael's program and his 401(k) plan in the event of divorce.

CASE STUDY 2. GIFT OF A HOME

Audrey, a dentist, and Tim, a principal of an Internet start-up, decide to get married. As a wedding present, Audrey's parents give them a three-bedroom house, relieving them of a major financial responsibility. Audrey and Tim enter into a prenup saying that in the event of divorce, Audrey keeps the entire house. Otherwise Tim could argue that a joint gift was made and that the house belongs to them equally. Or he might make a claim on the house based on his improvements to it and resulting appreciation in value. Without a prenup, there is little likelihood that Audrey would get the entire house—not exactly a palatable result for Audrey's parents or Audrey.

CASE STUDY 3. ANTICIPATED INHERITANCE

Paul is an aspiring screenwriter. Carol is an unpublished children's book writer. Paul supports himself from income from several trust funds and anticipates a substantial inheritance. Carol's assets are negligible.

Under the law of their state, if Paul kept his money completely separate and in his name only, Carol would not be entitled to any of the trust funds or inheritance if they divorced. If Paul's movie career didn't take off, there would be no "marital" property for Carol to share. Upon death, however, in their state Carol would be entitled to one-third of Paul's entire estate (other than funds in the trust).

Paul and Carol decide upon "escalator" clauses: Paul agrees to pay Carol graduated lump sums based on the years of marriage in the event of divorce or death. Carol waives her rights to spousal support, equitable distribution, and her rights to inherit from Paul's estate. In turn, Paul waives his rights to Carol's unpublished children's book on okapi and other exotic animals. (Could she be creating the next Harry Potter?)

The prenup enables Carol to pursue her career as a writer without fear that she will end up empty-handed if the marriage breaks up. For his part, Paul garners his parents' support for the marriage and ensures that family money stays in the family.

AROUND THE WORLD WITH PRENUPS

The global village extends even to prenups and postnups.

In Denmark, prenups have always been popular, according to Annelise Lemche, a lawyer in Copenhagen. To be enforceable there, prenups must be registered with the National Registry, which is akin to a Land Registry. The Registry has been in existence since the 1920s and is open to the public. Also in Sweden, marriage agreements must be registered in a Marriage Register in Orebro.

Inspired by the Scandinavian countries, in 1965 France instituted major matrimonial reform, based on the principle of freedom of spouses to adopt any system concerning their financial situation. According to the French INSEE (Institut National de la Sta-

CASE STUDY 4. PARTIAL PRENUP

Tom is a stockbroker. Sue is a flight attendant. Tom is a partner in a family limited partnership. His interest is worth about $250,000, although he does not have access to the money now. Tom and Sue live in a house that Sue inherited.

So-called DINKs (dual income, no kids), Tom and Sue have been living a carefree life. Other than Tom's limited partnership interest, they have no savings to

tistique et des Etudes Economiques), today about 19 percent of the population enter into a *contrat de mariage* (16 percent, before marriage; 3 percent, after marriage).

In Germany, prenups have been enforceable for over a century. When asked how often prenups are used, Werner U. Martens, a solicitor and matrimonial specialist in Munich, replied, "Not often enough." He estimates that about 20 percent of marriages have prenups.

In England and Australia, prenups are in an embryonic stage. They are not automatically binding on courts, although courts have an obligation to consider them as strong evidence. In both countries, the use of prenups is increasing, and movements are under way to bolster their legal status.

speak of, since they spend all their disposable income on travel, restaurants, clothing, and entertainment.

Tom and Sue have agreed to start a family in a few years. Sue does not know whether she will stop working. Tom and Sue cannot visualize what their life will be like then.

In a prenup, Sue waives her interest (including postmarriage appreciation) in the family partnership, and Tom waives his interest (including postmarriage appreciation) in Sue's house in the event of a divorce. In other areas, however, they agree not to agree. Thus, the prenup remains silent on questions of spousal support and property other than the family partnership and the house. Those issues seem too remote to deal with at this point. Perhaps they will enter into an agreement after marriage—a postnuptial or internuptial agreement—if and when their circumstances change. In agreeing not to agree in certain areas, they at least understand what issues they have and what laws apply.

CASE STUDY 5. THE OLD SWITCHEROO

An entrepreneur, Len has substantial family money in trusts and other vehicles. When he announces he wants to marry Tamayo, a penniless artist who lives in Japan, Len's parents convince him to enter into a prenup. Tamayo finds the agreement unfathomable, but ultimately acquiesces. She signs a prenup in which she and Len agree to keep their assets separate and mutually waive all claims against each other, with the exception of temporary maintenance for Tamayo if they divorce.

Len invests the overwhelming bulk of his fortune in a business shortly before the collapse of the Pacific Rim economy. Tamayo in the meantime studies computer animation and quickly becomes a hotshot in the field. At the time of their divorce, Len is heavily indebted, having personally guaranteed some business loans. Tamayo in the meantime moves to Los Angeles, works for Disney, stashes away a nice nest egg, and receives pay hikes with each new project. None of Tamayo's assets is exposed to Len's debts. The prenup that was originally written to protect Len has shielded Tamayo. She's writing a thank-you note to Len's parents.

Mature Couples in Remarriages and Mid-Careers

Case Study 1. Support Obligations

Maria is a caterer at a small company. Carlos is a foreman at a factory. Carlos was previously married and has support obligations to his first wife. Carlos doesn't want to expose Maria to any possible liability for payments of support to his ex-wife. For example, if the couple put their assets in joint name, their joint account might be subject to the support claims of Carlos's ex-wife. Maria and Carlos enter into a prenup, agreeing to keep their assets and earnings separate.

Case Study 2. Protecting the Less Well-Off

Deb and Trey are getting married. Trey is sixty-five years old and has had a successful career as a radio talk show host in the Midwest. He is about to retire. Deb is thirty-nine years old and is a photographer. In their state, property acquired prior to marriage is considered "separate" property and not divisible in divorce.

Although Deb has modest assets, she requests a prenuptial agreement. She wants to make sure that in the event of divorce, she receives some lump-sum settlement. Since Trey is retiring, he might not have any future earnings to divide. Trey is somewhat surprised—he didn't know the law and he thought that he was being *romantic* by not asking Deb for a prenuptial agreement. By precipitating the prenup, Deb asks Trey to be more generous than he otherwise would be required under the law. By agreeing to the proposed prenup, Trey shows his loving feelings toward Deb.

Case Study 3. No Prenup

Paul owns and operates a manufacturing plant. He was previously married and has two children. Paul has amassed about $350,000 in stocks and bonds, which he wants to protect for the benefit of his children.

Patsy is Paul's fiancée. She will not hear of a prenup. She feels that it is demeaning and insulting. Paul has done everything he can to convince her, including consulting a therapist. (Unfortunately, this book was not available at the time.)

Although Patsy has a block against the prenup, their relationship is otherwise sound and strong. Paul does not want to pressure Patsy to sign an agreement. He thinks about his objectives: He wants to protect his kids. Thus, he decides to utilize funds from his brokerage accounts to establish trusts for the benefit of his children. (Paul could also create a trust with premarital money for his own benefit in his state if he wanted.)

Paul tells Patsy that he is setting up these trusts for his children to ensure their welfare and Patsy is amenable. She knows how important Paul's children are to him. She also feels relieved that Paul has not insisted on the agreement.

Although Patsy and Paul do not enter into a prenup, they engage in a prenuptial dialogue. This enables them to identify and resolve their sources of conflict and concern prior to the marriage, thus putting them on a firmer foundation for the future. They thus enjoy some of the benefits of a prenup even though they ultimately don't sign one.

CASE STUDY 4. REMARRIAGE WITH A YOUNG CHILD

Bari had been a single divorced parent with a young child. After her bruising divorce, she ended up with very little financially. Ten years later, she has acquired her own home and some savings by working for the financial aid office of the state university. Determined not to repeat her mistakes, she enters into a prenup with Tyrone in which he waives all his rights to her assets, including her 403(b) annuity. Reciprocally, Bari gives up all rights to a laundry business that Tyrone owns at the time of marriage together with any appreciation in value during marriage. They agree to each sell their homes and buy a larger one, and in the event of divorce, each will get back what each put into the house, together with a pro rata share of appreciation.

Eight years later, Tyrone's business folds, Bari becomes the sole breadwinner, and the couple divorces. The prenup enables Bari to preserve her assets and protect her child's future.

CASE STUDY 5. REMARRIAGE WITH ADULT CHILDREN

Al and Louise plan to marry. Al, who is divorced with two sons from a previous marriage, has a successful car dealership and a summer cottage that he wants to leave to his sons. Al's sons are nervous about Louise's rights to such property. Louise's husband died from asbestosis, as a result of which she received a substantial settlement. Louise wants to ensure that the settlement passes to her daughters, who are paranoid that Al's sons will somehow end up with that money.

Without a prenup, both Al and Louise would each

have a right in their state to receive a certain percentage of the other's estate upon death. The settlement, the dealership, and cottage might be exposed to one another's claims in the event of divorce.

Thus, Al and Louise enter into a prenup in which they each waive all their rights to the other's assets. Since Al is wealthier than Louise, Al agrees to make annual contributions to a fund for Louise's benefit in the event of divorce or death. At the same time, he makes sure that the rest of his estate, including the dealership and cottage, passes directly to his sons. Likewise, Louise preserves for her daughters the monies received on account of their father's death.

Louise's and Al's children dance with each other at the wedding.

CASE STUDY 6. REMARRIAGE WITH ADULT GRANDCHILDREN

Sol, eighty-five years young, with a net worth in excess of $3 million, is marrying Bertha, eighty-one years young, with assets also in excess of $3 million. Each has a city apartment and a country home. Their biggest problem is how to consolidate their club memberships. They each waive all rights they have in each other's property in the event of death or divorce. For these octogenarians, life is just beginning. They don't forget about their past lives and arrange for their assets to pass directly to their five children, fourteen grandchildren, and seven great-grandchildren. God bless. They should live to be a hundred and twenty.

These cases describe real-life situations where prenups solved problems, reduced stress, and solidified marriages. They introduced dialogue that protected the relationships over time. They provided a bedrock foundation for marriage and brought the couples closer emotionally and rationally.

These case studies may help you realize that *you* have a lot to gain from entering into a prenup. They may give you some ideas about what you want to include in your prenup. The next section will show you how to bring the subject up and how to go about getting the agreement you want. Read on.

AUDIENCE APPLAUSE

TV sitcoms—a barometer of our pop culture— have featured prenups prominently in their story lines. In *Family Law,* a woman attorney fell for her male client who wanted a prenup to protect his future wife against his debts. "That's the sweetest reason I've ever heard for wanting a prenup," she said. In *The Nanny,* Miss Fine (Fran Drescher) melted when it turned out that the prenup proposed by Mr. Sheffield was in actuality adoption papers for his children. *Seinfeld, Ally McBeal,* and *Sex in the City* have devoted episodes to prenups. If we learn and laugh about prenups on prime-time TV, can their everyday use be far behind?

Part Two

What to Do

Before You Say

"I Do"

How to Do It

Chapter 5

BROACHING THE "P" WORD

*O*kay, you've decided that you want a prenup before you marry the love of your life. But now you want to know about popping the "P" word. This chapter gives you advice about when, where, and how and provides some tips on how to respond if your partner brings up the topic before you do.

WHEN?
GET YOUR PARTNER IN THE MOOD

It's a good idea to bring up the concept of a prenup as early as possible in the relationship—ideally while you are dating. At this point you might refer to an event in the news. For example, if the divorce of a high-profile couple like Ted Turner and Jane Fonda or Bruce Willis and Demi Moore is splashed across the headlines, you might work the topic of prenups into your discussion of current events. You can segue into a casual statement of your pro-prenup beliefs and try to elicit your date's views. This opens up discussion before things become very personal between you. If the discussion is ongoing, it smooths the way for later.

Similarly you might use the experience of a friend or a relative as a springboard for expressing your point of view. Or use this book. Tell your partner that some down-to-earth but romantic lawyer thinks all couples should get prenups. And one of her best arguments is that in the long run, it will keep you away from lawyers.

As you progress in the relationship, you may relate the prenup to your personal situation. If possible, you should have this discussion before mentioning the "M" word. But if the "M" word comes first, the "P" word should quickly follow. Ideally you should at least have the conversation before a public engagement is announced and before wedding plans are made.

Some suggest that the optimal time is after the initial blush of excitement over the engagement and before entering into other premarital contracts, such as the agreement with the caterer. This provides time for you and your sweetheart to work out any difficult issues that arise. And if the differences are irreconcilable, then you avoid embarrassment and expense.

WHERE?
CREATE THE RIGHT ATMOSPHERE

Some say a soft approach in an elegant restaurant is the best way. Others say at least it should be first mentioned in a public place—in case your intended reacts emotionally. Your car is probably not the safest place to bring up the topic.

Most advise discussion in a neutral place. Not in your office or bedroom. I'd suggest a quiet moment on the living-room sofa.

The atmosphere you create is all-important—keep it warm and loving.

HOW?
HAVE A HEART-TO-HEART

When you're close to the moment of truth, telling the truth is the best approach. If you're straightforward about a prenup, it bodes well for the marriage.

So you take a deep breath and broach the topic from a commonsensical standpoint. You need to raise your concerns as to *why* you want a prenup. Are you afraid of losing your life's savings or something of emotional value? Giving up something—tangible or intangible— for the marriage? Tell your partner *why* you want a prenup.

The idea is to invite discussion about the underlying issues at this point. You should not be concerned about decision making. You don't need to reach conclusions in your initial conversations. You should just talk

about the issues without any immediate pressure to resolve them.

Listen to the response carefully. What concerns are
you hearing back?

Have a long heart-to-heart. You should both be comfortable with *why* you are doing a prenup before you get
into the details.

GULP! HOW TO CHOOSE
YOUR WORDS

Although there are no magic words, here are some possible opening lines:

♥ "Let's talk about our future, what we both want,
our lifestyles, our present and future finances. I
want to make sure that all our money issues
are addressed and resolved up front. Then we
won't have them hanging over us when we get
married."

♥ "I'm really afraid of what happened to ———.
Let's take control of our lives and write our own
marriage contract. Then we can create our own
rules and regulations and not be at the mercy of
a judge who might be unfair to one of us."

♥ "I was badly burned in my divorce. I would like
to marry again, and I certainly don't expect to divorce again, but I have to be certain I never go
through an ugly scene like that again. I need to
know what will happen in advance if we ever
break up."

♥ "My children are very concerned about my marriage and what it might mean for their inheritance. I'm worried about this, too. Since most of my assets are from their father, they are entitled to those assets. They will be happier about this marriage if we do some estate planning. That will make me happier, too."

♥ "I believe that marriage is a fifty-fifty proposition, and I'm concerned about giving up my job to become a full-time mother and homemaker. I want to make sure that my contributions are valued even if they aren't tangible or monetary. Can we establish a principle of equal sharing at the outset?"

♥ "One of the things I have to consider before getting married is my family (or parents') business. I know the last thing we want to think about is that our marriage won't last, but I need to feel confident that the business remains in the family."

♥ "Darling, I'm worried about how my debts may affect your assets. I think it would be beneficial if we agreed to keep our property separate."

♥ "I worked very hard to acquire a nest egg, and I want to be sure that I will still have it in the unlikely event the unthinkable occurs between us."

♥ "I stand to inherit a cottage from my parents, which has been in the family for some time, and which has tremendous sentimental value to me. I need to know that the cottage will be protected if anything goes wrong in our marriage."

♥ "Honey, I love you, but what happens if one of us dies or we get divorced? Maybe we should at least discuss an agreement."

PRENUP NO-NOS: WHAT *NOT* TO DO

Don't *spring* a prenup on your intended. Don't present it as a fait accompli. Don't convey the impression "I don't trust you, I don't love you, I'm not sure we're going to make it, and I won't get married unless you sign it." Don't let your partner hear you say, "I don't want you to get my money."

Unfortunately, some people react negatively to the word *prenup*. Although undeserved, the "P" word may have a pejorative connotation to your intended and provoke an emotional reaction. That may have a chilling effect on substantive conversation. Therefore, it's important to prepare your partner so you don't catch him/her off guard or by surprise.

The right tone is essential. This is not the time to be imperious or patronizing. "Come here, snookums, I have something for you to sign" is premaritally incorrect. Although you might say, "It is necessary for me," avoid such threatening ultimatums as "You have to sign it," or "I won't get married without it."

❧

YOUR PRENUP IS A TWO-WAY STREET

It's important to stress that although *you* may be initiating the prenup conversation, the agreement needs to be *mutual.*

You should tell your partner that you believe that a prenup is a positive thing. You believe it encourages openness and honesty and furthers dialogue and dispute resolution. You feel it is a sign of trust because both

RAISING RED FLAGS

Your partner's prenup behavior is inappropriate and unacceptable if he/she:

1. Presents the prenup for the first time immediately before the wedding, for example, at the rehearsal dinner or the church altar.

2. Asks you to stop off at a lawyer's office to sign a routine document (i.e., the prenup) that you have not previously seen.

3. Tells you that you don't need a lawyer and that his/her lawyer will look after both of you.

4. Advises you to sign on the dotted line even though you haven't read the prenuptial agreement.

5. Promises you that the prenup will be revised or ripped up *after* the wedding.

of you make full and frank disclosure. Your view is that it puts the marriage on a solid footing.

Further, you intend to be fair and reasonable. You will not take advantage or exploit each other. Each of you will be active participants in the negotiation process. The agreement will be a joint effort. You will complete the prenup well in advance of the honeymoon. And you hope that your prenup, like an insurance policy, will lie fallow in your file cabinet.

Above all, you *both* have input and provide feedback. Your prenup is *not* a unilateral, one-sided document. Rather, it is the product of give-and-take between you. You each express your opinions and you listen to each other. You each will have the opportunity to say, "This is important to me," or "This doesn't work for me."

WHY NOT BLAME YOUR LAWYER?

Some persons advise pointing a finger at your lawyer, accountant, financial adviser, friend, parents, or children. I'd be wary of this approach. Although it might initially ease the tension between you, there are dangers. For instance, when blaming family members, you need to be especially tactful. Otherwise you can unwittingly engender resentment between your spouse and family members.

And you must be cautious about your "white lies." For example, you could get into trouble if your spouse discovers after marriage that other in-laws did not sign prenups.

One school of thought, the so-called Dale Carnegie approach, is to describe the problem and ask your partner how he/she thinks it can be resolved. He/she might come up with the prenup solution on his/her own. Or you can draw it out of him/her by asking, "Do you think some kind of agreement might take care of this?"

KEEP IT COOL

If initially you don't get a receptive response from your intended, try to explain your reason, saying that you want to avoid or clarify an issue before it becomes a problem in the relationship. If you encounter anger or hostility, back off. Give your partner time to think. Hand him/her this book. Ask your partner to consult with colleagues, friends, advisers. Try again at a calmer moment. Rephrase. Pressuring your partner into signing a prenup is not a good way to start a marriage.

Also watch out for passive-aggressive responses. These are statements that seem to be compliant, but veil anger or hostility. "Anything you want." "You go ahead and draft it." Try to elicit discussion by saying, "What are your suggestions? Are you angry about it? Talk to me about it." Your partner's reaction may be symptomatic of a communication problem. If you do not resolve this problem now, you are most likely going to encounter it again the next time an issue arises in your relationship.

If you make a prenup a sticking point, it may become more and more divisive. Keep the conversation free and open. Use "I" statements or phrases that describe *your own* needs and desires ("I'm worried about . . ." or "I feel scared that . . ."), but that don't accuse.

You should make sure that both you and your partner are ultimately satisfied with the terms of your prenup. If you or your partner are unhappy, it can be a source of resentment later.

How to Respond to the "P" Word

But what if *you're* being asked to agree to a prenup?

At this point, you may feel insecure or anxious about your own financial predicament. On the other hand, you may not want to appear greedy. You may be concerned about your partner's depth of commitment. You may fear putting the relationship at risk or finding out things about your partner that you did not know.

You may feel that you have no choice but to accept the "terms" of the proffered prenup. If you have a *Pretty Woman* fantasy that a spouse will make you safe and secure, you may be confused.

Act rationally, not emotionally. Chill. Listen *carefully* to what your partner is saying. Try to *understand* fully what your partner wants and why he/she wants it. If he/she is not saying *why*, ask. *Focus* on the content of what your partner is saying. Is it reasonable? Do you need clarification? Do you need more information? What questions do you have? Ask those questions. Try to have a normal, modulated discussion about the substance of what your partner is proposing.

Try not to feel pressure to agree or disagree with your partner at the outset. When the "P" word is broached, your partner is *initiating* a dialogue. He/she is not presenting a document that is about to be signed, sealed, and delivered. He/she is presenting an idea that needs to be developed and implemented by the two of you over a period of time.

No-Nos: How Not to Respond

At this stage, you don't make any decisions; you are discussing your concerns, your feelings, your fears, your dreams. Don't feel forced to arrive at any conclusions.

Don't say, "You can take your engagement ring and shove it." Don't storm out of the room. Don't say, "If you want to discuss it, have your lawyer speak to my lawyer."

Also don't say, "I thought you loved me. I thought you trusted me. I thought we were in this forever." Followed by tears or sulks.

And also don't say, "Whatever you want, honey. I'll

You Could Look It Up

According to a dictionary that compiled the new words of the twentieth century, the term "prenuptial agreement" dates to 1910.

sign whatever. I'm not after your money. I just want you to be happy." Followed by the silent treatment.

Prenuptus Interruptus

After the initial conversation, a good approach is to table the discussion and take a time-out.

Once things are quieter, think about whether your partner's request makes sense to you. What part do you agree with? What part doesn't sound right to you? What are your concerns? You want to set up a two-way dialogue and see the prenup as something that you, too, may have a stake in. Think about what you'd like from the agreement. And think about what you'd like to cover.

Chapter 6

WHAT TO COVER
(OR UNCOVER)
IN YOUR PRENUP

℘

A CHECKLIST

*S*o you've now discussed a prenup in the abstract. This chapter takes you from a general conversation to the specific areas you can cover in your prenup.

You may opt to cover as many or as few issues as you like. You probably will not cover every one of the items I've listed. Some may not be relevant or important to you. And you may include items I haven't indicated here (such as lifestyle issues). But if you follow the list, you'll be sure that you have considered the key issues that may be handled in a prenuptial agreement:

1. List your assets, liabilities, income, and expectations of gifts and inheritances.

2. Provide how premarital and post-marital debts will be paid.

3. Agree upon what happens to your *premarital* property—and *post*-marriage appreciation, gains, income, rentals, dividends, and proceeds of such property—in the event of death or divorce.

4. Agree upon what happens to your *post-marital* property in the event of death or divorce.

5. Determine ownership of your marital residence and secondary homes in the event of death or divorce.

6. Decide upon the status of gifts, inheritances, and trusts either spouse receives or benefits from, whether before or after marriage.

7. Select the beneficiary of all 401(k), 403(b), profit-sharing, pension, IRA, and all other retirement plans upon death and state if such benefits will be divided in the event of divorce.

8. Clarify what will happen to *each* type of property, whether jointly or individually owned, such as real estate, artwork, antiques, jewelry, earnings from employment or self-employment, stock options, stocks, bonds, mutual funds, businesses, professional practices, professional licenses or degrees, celebrity, goodwill, contracts, patents and copyrights, accident settlements, and winnings.

9. Figure out alimony, maintenance, or spousal support, or provide for a waiver or property settlement in-

stead of support (to the extent allowable by your state law).

10. Detail death benefits, stating what you will provide for in your will and the effect on state-mandated rights, such as "elective share" and "intestate" amounts.

11. Determine whether you wish your spouse to be an executor of your estate or trustee of any trust.

12. Decide upon medical, disability, life, or long-term-care insurance coverage.

13. Identify your attorneys.

14. Determine what state's law will apply and how your agreement will be affected by a move to another state.

15. Provide for child support or custody (although nonbinding).

Chapter 7

HOW TO BULLETPROOF YOUR PRENUP

ocial and demographic changes that began in the last quarter of the twentieth century have set the stage for the proliferation of prenups in the twenty-first. Greater information and education about their utility will popularize them even further and lead to widespread use. The prenups are indeed coming. This wave isn't to be feared, but welcomed. What may be unwelcome is an attack on your prenup by your partner. Although prenups overwhelmingly stand up in court, you don't want *yours* to be shot down. Here are some surefire actions you can take to bulletproof your prenup:

Start with a Legal Script

Movie mogul Steven Spielberg and actress Amy Irving directed and produced their own handwritten prenup in 1985. When Steven left her four years later for Kate Capshaw, Amy argued that she wasn't represented by a lawyer when she signed. The judge agreed with Amy, who received $100 million. Fortunately for Steven, *Jurassic Park, Schindler's List,* and *Saving Private Ryan* were ahead of him. For the rest of us, income replacement might not be that simple. In any event, Steven seemed to have learned his lesson. His marriage to Kate was preceded by a carefully scripted prenuptial agreement.

- ♥ Hire separate, independent counsel.
- ♥ Disclose your assets and liabilities.
- ♥ Allow yourself ample time.

Separate and Independent Counsel

There is no such thing as a do-it-yourself prenup.

A key step you can take to ensure the validity of your prenup is for you and your partner to hire separate and independent counsel.

In essence, a prenup is valid if you enter into it "voluntarily," without "coercion," and you have "knowledge" of the consequences of your actions. Also the agreement can't be "unconscionable"—manifestly unfair or one-sided. The proper use of separate and independent attorneys negates virtually all claims that a prenup is involuntary, coerced, unknowing, or unconscionable.

In most states, it is *not* an absolute requirement that you hire counsel. But if you don't, you imperil your prenup, because you don't have the requisite training, let alone objectivity. Thus, the old proverb: One who is his/her own lawyer has a fool for a client.

FINDING THE RIGHT LAWYER

How do you find a competent attorney? A time-honored method is to obtain a recommendation from a satisfied customer or a referral from a local bar association. You might ask a trusted attorney whom you've worked with for a suggestion. It's a good idea to interview a few possibilities so you can select an attorney with whom you have rapport and feel comfortable. Make sure the attorney has expertise in the area. Ask how long he/she has been writing prenuptial agreements, how many he/she has done, and whether he/she knows family law in addition to contracts and trusts and estates law.

Your attorney's style should be conciliatory, not confrontational. The process should not be *adversarial*. There is no winner or loser in this situation. You and your partner want to arrive at a compromise. Your attorney should act as an advocate and adviser, *not* as a prosecutor.

DON'T CREATE A CONFLICT OF INTEREST

To avoid charges of conspiracy, or as lawyers say, "conflict of interest," you and your partner each should independently choose your own attorney. This means you each find an attorney on your own. Neither you nor your attorney should refer your partner to an attorney. If possible, you should each pay your own attorney's fees.

You shouldn't go as a couple to a single attorney, even if you regard him/her as your "family attorney." Your attorney shouldn't attempt to explain the provisions of the prenup to your partner. That's your partner's attorney's job. The lines of communication are as follows: You speak to your attorney and your partner; your partner speaks to you and his/her attorney. The attorneys speak to each other and their respective clients.

By hiring separate, independent counsel, you each have your own attorney to explain your rights and obligations under the laws of your states. In this way, you can see what you're getting and what you're giving up, both with and without a prenup, and you are in a position to reach an even-handed agreement. Some lawyers will provide you with a separate document, comparing and contrasting what you are entitled to under the law of the state versus what you are entitled to under the proposed prenup.

In addition, counsel will guide you so your emotions don't get the better of you. The natural tendency is for engaged couples to defer to each other. Your attorney's job is to make sure that your loving feelings don't compromise the fairness of the document.

BE WISE

You may never have hired an attorney before. You simply may be attorney-averse and may view a visit to your lawyer as welcome as having your wisdom teeth extracted.

Just keep in mind, if you're wary of going to a lawyer's office: If the unthinkable happens, you'll spend a lot less time in lawyers' offices once you have that precious prenup.

Although the prospect of you and your partner paying for not only Larry the Lawyer but also Anita the Attorney may be distasteful, a far worse scenario is having your agreement overturned. Would you save money by discontinuing your health insurance?

WHAT PRICE A PRENUP?

Keep in mind that you don't need to hire a high-profile lawyer who charges $500 an hour. Make sure you understand in advance your attorney's fee structure—whether you will be charged for the project or on an hourly basis. Just as some attorneys do a simple will, house closing, or divorce for a relatively low flat fee, some are willing to do a simple prenup for a fixed, affordable amount.

If your attorney charges an hourly rate for a more sophisticated prenup, you should get an estimate of what the total fee will be. The attorney will likely quote you a range and give you a disclaimer that the range could change if any complications develop. But at least you have a ballpark figure.

It is a common practice in the matrimonial field for an attorney to request a retainer. If your attorney asks you for a retainer, you will need a retainer agreement. You should read it carefully and make sure that it entitles you to terminate the attorney at any time and obtain a refund of any unused funds if the attorney has not rendered you services equal to the retainer amount.

BARRY BONDS HITS A HOMER

In 1988 San Francisco Giants baseball star Barry Bonds and his Swedish fiancée Susann (Sun), who was a bartender and cosmetology student, signed a prenuptial agreement the day before they married. Sun, then twenty-three and a recent immigrant, was accompanied only by a visiting Swedish friend. Barry, on the other hand, was advised by two attorneys.

At the time, Barry had just broken into the major leagues and was earning about $106,000 a year. When the prenup was challenged in 1994, Barry was earning $8 million a year. Sun did not work during the marriage, and the couple had two children. The agreement provided that Barry's earnings during the marriage would remain his separate property in the event of divorce.

A typical flat rate ranges from $150 to $3,000; a customary hourly rate ranges from $75 to $300. In major metropolitan areas, fees could be higher.

DO YOUR HOMEWORK

You can significantly cut down on the cost of a prenup, or any legal service for that matter, by doing your homework. Be proactive by researching the issues by yourself. By reading this book, you are doing pre-

Showing its predilection toward prenuptial agreements, the Supreme Court of California in August 2000 upheld the Bondses' agreement. The trial court had first validated the prenup, but that decision was overturned by the intermediate level Court of Appeal, only to be reversed by California's high court. The Supreme Court found that the agreement was voluntarily and knowingly entered into despite Sun's lack of representation. It added that Sun was under no pressure to proceed, because the wedding was "impromptu."

Providing advice for those who do not want to fight their cases for years and for those who may be not as lucky in litigation as Barry, California's high court said: "[O]bviously, the best assurance of enforceability is independent representation for both parties."

cisely that. You are familiarizing yourself with the concepts and terminology relating to a prenup. You know the look and lingo of a prenup. When you work with your attorney, you'll be able to use his or her time efficiently by not requiring your lawyer to teach you (and charge you for) Prenups 101. In addition, you will be a smarter client and might raise some points that are not in your attorney's regular repertoire.

The M.O. is that one attorney drafts a prenup on behalf of the person who initially requested the agreement, and the other attorney reviews that draft. The review shouldn't cost as much as the initial draft. Obviously, the more you and your partner work out the terms yourselves and stick to them, the less expense to you. You shouldn't hesitate, of course, to actively seek advice from your attorney, but be careful not to *waste* time and money.

To be efficient, you should use your attorney for legal, rather than therapeutic purposes. The temptation in prenuptial matters is to use your attorney as a sounding board, a friend, and a therapist. Attorneys don't have a special cut rate for "hand-holding" and charge you the same hourly rate whether the counseling provided is legal or otherwise. Consequently, those matters that can be hashed out with your mother, your sister, your best friend, or your barber/hairdresser don't need to be taken up with your attorney.

PROPERTY IS A PROPER ISSUE

Another way to save legal fees is to limit your prenup to property issues. As discussed in chapter 10, question 12, some people like to address so-called lifestyle issues in their prenups as well. These relate to serious matters such as career choice and place of residence and lighter points such as who will walk the dog and take out the garbage and how often you will go to the country or out to dinner.

Although communication is critical for both property and lifestyle concerns, only property provisions are *legally enforceable.* Provisions on lifestyle are only *morally persuasive.* Thus, my advice would be to focus on property issues with your attorney and work out the lifestyle issues with your partner, perhaps in a separate agreement—a love letter, if you will.

THE HEIRESS AND THE PLAYBOY

In 1947, tobacco heiress Doris Duke, considered the richest woman in America at the time, insisted that her bridegroom, international playboy Porfirio Rubirosa, sign a premarital agreement virtually at the altar. (Some reports indicated he fainted when he read it; another rumor claimed he was drugged.) In any event, he recovered in time to sign the prenup, proceed with the ceremony, and receive a house in Paris as a wedding gift.

The agreement that supposedly made "Rubi" faint called for him to receive an income of a paltry $25,000 a year. But he was given more than a million dollars and his own plane by the time they were divorced a year later. They parted friends and Doris continued to give him money and gifts after their divorce. It was also reported that their sex life did not end with the breakup of their marriage, although it was never revealed whether that was part of the prenup.

MAKE A GOOD INVESTMENT

In response to the skeptics who might consider advice from an attorney to hire an attorney self-serving: The widespread use of prenups is likely to reduce the volume of matrimonial law work, currently estimated at an aggregate of $28 billion each year. The cost of divorce far exceeds the cost of a prenup—some estimate by up to a thousand times! Moreover, the exercise of entering into a prenup inevitably will deter some from entering into marriage, usually those who shouldn't have gotten married in the first place, thus preventing divorces (and reducing legal fees).

The mere presence of separate, independent counsel will not 100 percent guarantee enforcement of a prenup. (For example, it may not be satisfactory to hire counsel at the last moment merely to rubber stamp the prenup.) However, the engagement of separate, independent counsel, each acting as an advocate, is far and away the best way to protect your prenup.

If you nevertheless decide not to engage counsel, you should have the appropriate language in the prenup that you were advised to seek separate, independent counsel, had the opportunity to do so, but declined to be represented after careful consideration. If you are not represented, you should be prepared to acknowledge that your partner's lawyer represents only your partner; that your interest and that of your partner likely will conflict; and that the lawyer is *not* protecting *you* or providing *you* with legal advice regarding your current or possible future circumstances.

FULL AND FRANK FINANCIAL DISCLOSURE

I'll show you mine, if you show me yours. This is the gist of premarital asset disclosure.

In a prenup, as well as in love, honesty is the best

policy. To protect your prenup, you must provide "full and fair" or "fair and reasonable" disclosure of your assets and liabilities. Why? A waiver of a right is valid only if you know what you're giving up. Usually you comply with this requirement by attaching to the prenup a signed schedule that completely describes your financial liabilities and your assets, together with actual or approximate values as of a recent date. An asset-by-asset inventory is best.

You should also include your annual income. If you have an expectation of a gift or inheritance or a substantial increase in income, you should reveal that as well.

In some states, financial disclosure is not an absolute requirement if the agreement is otherwise fair or not unconscionable. However, whether an agreement is otherwise fair and not unconscionable is a subjective determination. Further, under these circumstances, you usually must demonstrate that your partner knew or reasonably could have known of your financial position or that your partner voluntarily and expressly waived any right to disclosure. The problem is the difficulty of proving the requisite knowledge or voluntariness.

LET IT ALL HANG OUT

If you have accumulated wealth, you may experience difficulty in disclosing the full extent of your net worth. You may have acquired wealth by being thrifty, and you may feel that the disclosure of your wealth might encourage your partner to be extravagant. Or you may feel that your net worth is a state secret, a private matter not to be shared with another soul, and is, very plainly, no one else's beeswax.

The temptation in these situations might be to

downplay the value of certain assets or even omit them entirely. Like the tendency to lean back on your skis, your natural instinct here is the opposite of what you should do. You should disclose everything, and when in doubt, overstate rather than understate the value of the assets. This is because your partner's waiver must be knowing, and your partner cannot waive what he/she doesn't know about. An unknowing waiver has no legal effect, and it can be overturned if your partner chooses to push the point.

Also it may be possible that you live above your means and that you feel you will disappoint your sweetheart or that he/she will be scared off by your debts. If so, you should welcome the prenup as the moment of truth. As you are on the brink of an economic partnership, you can plan in advance how you will be paying off your debts and budgeting the family expenses (see chapter 8). Further, your lower net worth will enable you to negotiate a proportionate settlement in the prenup in the event of divorce.

If you inadvertently omit an asset, or unintentionally undervalue an asset, in the absence of fraud, you will not void the prenup as long as you present a substantially accurate picture of your financial holdings.

GET YOURSELF TOGETHER

Aside from shielding your prenup, an inventory provides a way to keep an accurate record of the assets you bring into the marriage. In many states, if you acquire property before your marriage, that property is considered "separate," not "marital," property, and the value is not divisible in the event of divorce. Unfortunately, at the time of divorce it is usually very difficult to prove which assets are separate and which are marital. This is because most assets get mixed together, or "commingled," and it is impossible to "trace" assets to their separate origin. Generally, property is presumed to be marital unless proven otherwise. The listing of assets annexed to the prenup can offer specific proof that property is separate.

Further, hidden assets can be a problem in divorce. The prenuptial statement of assets at least gives you a jumping-off point for comparison.

LEAD TIME BEFORE
THE WEDDING

In a perfect world, you begin working on a prenup months before the wedding. The prenuptial process should begin when you first talk about marriage, preferably before a public engagement (see chapter 5). This provides you and your partner with ample time to identify and elucidate the issues, select and meet with lawyers, negotiate solutions, review and revise drafts, prepare financial disclosure schedules, and sign the agreement.

Why is it that prenups are sometimes proposed at the rehearsal dinner? Usually the cause is not arrogance, but avoidance. This type of procrastination not only puts the prenup at risk but also threatens the viability of your relationship. If you have something important to say to your intended, you should get into the habit of saying it sooner rather than later.

In general, the law does not prescribe a specific time limit (although Minnesota requires you to sign prior to the day of marriage). The more time between the execution of the prenup and the marriage ceremony, though, the better protected you are. *You should aim for completion no later than thirty days before the ceremony.*

DON'T RUSH YOUR PRENUP

Some believe that the ideal time for completion is prior to sending out the invitations to the wedding. This target time causes the least amount of embarrassment in the event the wedding is washed out.

If you allow sufficient time, you prevent claims of involuntariness, duress, or coercion. If you present a prenup to your beloved the day or the week before the wedding, you are not giving your partner an adequate opportunity to consider it, to hire a lawyer, to have input, and to work toward a negotiated agreement. You have plenty else to think about and may not even comprehend what you're reading. You've mailed the invitations, you've fitted the wedding gown, you've made the final payment on the reception, and the guests are arriving from out of town. You're under considerable emotional, not to mention financial, pressure to proceed.

The timing rule has the salutary side effect of slowing down the premarital process—to make sure you are absolutely certain that your partner is your soul mate. Also, by completing the prenup well in advance of the wedding date, you've eliminated a possible distraction and allowed yourself the opportunity to fully savor the joys of your upcoming union.

Once again, there is no hard-and-fast rule on timing. A prenup for a last-minute Louie and Louise might be upheld if they were both sophisticated and educated, and each consulted with separate, independent counsel. This is particularly true if they fully considered the document in advance of the wedding, but just didn't get around to signing it until close to the wedding.

As a general rule, if the timing is short, the prenup is precarious. Not to mention boorish. Be a class act and get your prenup together . . . well in advance of your wedding.

THE TRUMP PRENUP AND ITS PROGENY

The Donald has emblazoned his name on prenups, just as he has on buildings in New York and Atlantic City. Because of his insistence on prenups and his persistence in enforcing them, he has demonstrated to the world their effectiveness and enforceability.

PART ONE: THE DONALD AND THE IVANA

Real estate mogul Donald Trump made his mark as a successful *developer*. In his personal life, however, he achieved fame as the consummate *dissolver*. He helped popularize the premarital agreement in 1977 when he entered into one with Ivana Winkelmayr, former Olympic skier and Czechoslovakian fashion model. They updated it three times during the marriage.

In 1990, Donald announced he and Ivana were divorcing. The prenup provided that she would receive "only" about $25 million.

Ivana claimed that she played a big part in building and running the Trump empire as well as being Trump's wife for twelve years and the mother of his three children. She argued that she should receive half of his fortune of somewhere between $1.7 billion and $4 billion and that she would not have reaffirmed the agreement in 1987 if she had been aware of his "adultery and philandering" (see Part Two below).

Ivana ended up with roughly what was promised in the prenup: $10 million; a $4 million housing allowance if she left the Trump Tower triplex; the mansion in Greenwich, Connecticut; use of the Mar-a-Lago estate in Palm Beach, Florida, for one month a year, plus $650,000 a year in support.

PART TWO: THE DONALD AND THE MARLA

Donald and Marla Maples married in 1992 and separated in 1997, just shy of a milestone that would have upped the settlement. The prenup was upheld, providing Marla with $2 million, plus nanny costs, tuition, and expenses for daughter Tiffany. At the time of the divorce, The Donald's net worth was estimated at between $2.5 and $5 billion.

PART THREE: THE IVANA AND RICCARDO

At the time of their 1995 wedding, Ivana's net worth had grown to about $45 million (see Part One above), while Italian businessman Riccardo Mazzucchelli was worth about $10 million. Their prenup essentially provided that hers was hers and his was his. Three years later, when they divorced, there was no exchange of assets. Thus, Ivana's settlement from The Donald remained intact.

The Trumps provide some pointers for others to follow. The Donald, in his best-selling book *Trump: The Art of the Comeback,* advises: "Be paranoid. Be lucky. Get even. Have a prenuptial agreement." His first wife, Ivana, may have summed up her philosophy in a line of dialogue she uttered as an actress in the movie *The First Wives Club:* "Don't get mad, get everything."

Chapter 8

PREMARITAL FINANCIAL PLANNING

&

FOR RICHER OR RICHER

t's no secret that couples argue about money more than any other topic. Seventy percent of divorces are caused by money matters—even more than by sex and in-laws. In the financial planning community, conventional wisdom is that the solution to this problem is communication during courtship, optimally at least six months before marriage. You should know each other's fiscal (that's fiscal, *not* physical) profile before you say your vows—a simple prophylactic measure. Nevertheless, most couples usually first talk about money two weeks to two months after marriage. Which is much too late.

The prenuptial agreement is an ideal vehicle to facilitate the proper disclosure and discussion of vital money matters. You deal systematically with relevant issues so you don't overlook them. You come to an understanding that you memorialize in writing. From this understanding, you are able to develop a financial plan. You both feel more protected and prepared when you walk down the aisle. You are able to approach the practical aspects of your marriage in a constructive manner and thus lay the foundation for a financially sound—even prosperous—marriage.

PLANNERS PREFER PRENUPS

Financial planners from all over the country generally welcome prenups as a way to confront money issues, arrange financial affairs, and solve problems before marriage.

Peter Haas Calfee, CFP, CPA, CLU, AEP, Calfee Financial Advisors Inc., Cleveland, Ohio: "I often suggest a prenuptial as a means of exploring a lot of other issues in advance of the union. It becomes a means to an end, where the end is communication. It enables a couple to focus on the larger issues: how they view money, how they view wealth and their lifestyle needs, and how they view themselves and the dispensation of funds."

Susan Freed, CFP, Susan Freed & Associates, Washington, D.C., agrees: "Prenuptials are healthy. Money is really the last taboo, and people don't want to talk about it."

With respect to any negative perception, Sally Bliss, financial adviser and vice president of a major investment firm, says: "I think that prenups have become more sophisticated and are being used, in my mind, for more and more of the right reasons. Prenups can be very helpful in a new relationship. You don't have issues because they have been dealt with already."

Marianne Shine, CFP, CDP, Shine Financial Inc.,

Deerfield Beach, Florida, points out that a prenuptial agreement is based upon openness. "The chief advantage in my opinion is to avoid miscommunication and misunderstanding where one is assuming this and the other is presuming this, but the couple never talked about it so they don't know that they don't have the same understanding. . . . A prenuptial could bring issues to the forefront in a way that might not otherwise be brought out."

DISCLOSURE OF ASSETS AND DEBTS

Before you marry, planners suggest you should exchange your net worth, your assets, your liabilities, your income, and your expenses. You don't actually have to get out the pay stubs, credit reports, tax returns, and balance sheets, although it's probably not a bad idea. You need to figure out your collective income and your collective expenses.

If you are paying alimony, child support, or college tuition, or if you are supporting an aging parent, you need to share that information. If you have any significant debts, personal bankruptcy, or negative credit card history, you want to divulge this before marriage. You don't want your spouse to be surprised if your first joint credit card application is rejected.

Ms. Shine points out that the prenuptial agreement provides a "structure" for premarital financial planning. "Most people are disorganized. A crucial aspect of financial planning is that it needs to be in writing because that makes it real. And one of the advantages of a prenuptial agreement is that it is in writing and therefore it is real and you know where you stand."

Prenups are most problematical, Ms. Freed says,

when "one party is secretive by nature and avoids deal-ing with money issues." Ironically, "the people who put up the most resistance, who are the hardest to reach, often are the ones who need prenuptial agreements the most," she says.

DISCUSSION OF FINANCIAL GOALS AND MONEY PERSONALITIES

In addition to exchanging "hard" information about each other, financial planners recommend that you should discuss, well in advance of the marriage date, your financial goals and money personalities.

FINANCIAL GOALS

Specifically, here are some of the myriad money topics you might discuss, some of which you probably covered in the getting-to-know-you stage of your rela-tionship:

- ♥ What kind of lifestyle are you aiming for?
- ♥ How many children do you want?
- ♥ Will you both continue working?
- ♥ What are your short-term goals? A down pay-ment on a car or a home? furniture? vacation? getting out of debt?
- ♥ What are your long-term goals? Starting a fam-ily? vacation home? college tuition? retirement?
- ♥ How much will you be spending and how much will you be saving? How much will be used to pay off debt?

- ♥ What is your tolerance for indebtedness?
- ♥ What investment strategy will you adopt to achieve your goals? Are you conservative or aggressive?
- ♥ How will you provide for your children from a prior marriage, aging parents, or other dependents?

MONEY PERSONALITY

To determine one another's money personality, discuss your perception of the value of money and material goods. You should try to unravel the emotional strings that are tied to money.

Your family history is relevant here. Here are some possible topics to cover:

- ♥ Did you come from a home where your parents gave you everything you wanted?
- ♥ Did both your parents work?
- ♥ Were your parents financially successful?
- ♥ Did you come from a background of chronic underemployment and overextension?
- ♥ Did your parents own a business that was affected by downturns in the economy?
- ♥ Was your mother a single parent?
- ♥ Was your father the principal breadwinner?
- ♥ Did your mother go on shopping trips when she was depressed?
- ♥ Was your father a compulsive gambler?
- ♥ Did your father think that every paycheck was his last?
- ♥ Did your parents suffer reversals of fortune?

MONEY PROFILE

What is your money profile? These are some of the possibilities:

- ♥ Do you look at money as a matter of security?
- ♥ Does money represent freedom and independence?
- ♥ Does money make you feel more powerful?
- ♥ Do you use money to improve your relationships with others?

SAVER VERSUS SPENDER

Are you a saver or a spender? Studies say that eight out of ten times a saver is married to a spender. It's more than just that opposites attract. A saver doesn't want to be bored to death by marrying another saver. A spender usually avoids a combustible combo with another spender. Consequently, the saver usually clicks with a spender. Thus, in the usual saver-spender match, the couple inevitably has to negotiate and work out a compromise on how they are going to live.

Even in a saver-saver match or a spender-spender match, the money personalities in the couple tend to polarize, so that one becomes the saver or spender relative to the other. Or they can enter into a competition, where one tries to outsave or outspend the other.

There is hardly a divorce more bitter than when a saver has saved all of his/her assets, the spender has squandered all of his/her assets, and then the saver has to fork over a percentage of his/her assets to the spender as a property settlement.

Financial Revelations

As Ms. Bliss points out: "I think the discussion of money can provoke something that you haven't seen before, which in my view is a good thing. . . . People are funny when it comes to money. People can be the most rational, honest, forthright, considerate, generous people in the world and then all of a sudden the word *money* is thrown in there, and people change."

Take the following two instances, each involving a man with multiple millions entering into a prenuptial agreement with a woman of modest means. In one case, the woman insisted on a transfer of property immediately following the marriage. Was she marrying for money? In the other case, the man insisted upon the daily accrual of monetary penalties if his partner failed to comply with the agreement. Was he a control freak? In both cases, the man and woman married—but with their eyes *open*.

Development of a Financial Plan

Identification of Whom You Want to Protect

You have to determine what you want your money to do for you and those you want to take care of. Who is in your family? What does the family consist of? How many children? How many ex-spouses? If you are a young couple and want to have children, you must obviously take that into consideration.

Not to be overlooked today as a component of the family is a parent. Parents of the baby boom generation are living longer. American families spent $24 billion for the care of elderly parents in 1998.

His, Hers, and Ours

You have to figure out what assets and income are his, what are hers, and what are ours. Similarly you have to determine which expenses are individual and which are joint. You then agree what assets and income will be used to take care of which expenses. If there is any debt, you clarify how that will be paid. Your decisions can be reflected in a prenup.

One recommended approach is the establishment of HIS, HERS, and OURS bank accounts and credit cards. You each have your own bank account and credit card, and you also have a joint bank account and joint credit card. The system not only provides the parties with individuality, but also a structure for determining how each account will be funded and which expenses will be paid out of each account.

Separate credit cards provide each of you an independent credit rating, which can be important in a business venture or in the event of death or divorce. The joint accounts and cards typically fund household, vacation, and insurance expenses. The individual accounts and cards typically are used for clothes, hobbies, gifts, and entertainment.

Other expenses would have to be decided. For example, if there are student, credit, or IRS debts, from which accounts will they be paid? If there are obligations to children, parents, ex-spouses, or other relatives, how will these expenses be paid? Also, how much will each contribute to the joint account? Will the joint account be used to fund some "individual" expenses of the

Six Steps of Premarital Financial Planning

Marianne Shine, CFP, CDP, Shine Financial Inc., Deerfield Beach, Florida, feels that prenuptials dovetail well with a six-step process of financial planning that should be used at every major life stage:

- ♥ Discussing financial goals for the short-term, medium-term, and long-term—what's the money for, when do you need it, and how much do you need
- ♥ Disclosing assets and liabilities—what you have and what you have to work with
- ♥ Evaluating what it all means—what are your strengths and weaknesses
- ♥ Developing a plan to use what you have most effectively to accomplish what you want
- ♥ Implementing the plan
- ♥ Updating the plan to respond to changes in your personal life, the economy, markets, tax laws, and investment performance

other party? Typically, couples with disparity in wealth "adjust" in this fashion. The wealthier party contributes a greater amount to the joint account, which benefits both parties.

But remember: Your financial planning should be on a macro basis. Don't micromanage every minor expense. You don't want to account for every milk carton.

SEPARATION OF ASSETS

There are several standard reasons for keeping assets in separate names:

- ♥ one party is in debt
- ♥ one party faces a threat of a lawsuit
- ♥ one party's assets are being used to guarantee business debts
- ♥ one party is in a high-risk business situation
- ♥ one party receives assets from his/her family
- ♥ for estate planning
- ♥ for keeping assets distinct for children from a prior marriage
- ♥ for consistency with a prenuptial agreement

EXAMPLES: PRENUPS IN FINANCIAL PLANNING

Example: An accountant meets a real estate broker at a party and within a few months they decide to marry. The politically incorrect accountant tells his friends he likes the line of her bottom, but not her bottom line. As a fiscal conservative, he loves everything about her except her shopping habits. In the prenuptial process, the man discovers that his fiancée has no assets, but Visa debt in excess of $12,000. The couple agrees to keep their assets separate and not assume responsibility for each other's debts, unless they specifically agree otherwise. They also work out a "spending" plan. Through communication and premarital contracting, they have protected themselves against credit card catastrophe.

Example: A man is interested in protecting his new wife as well as his three grown children. By taking the man's assets and running them through various scenarios, assuming retirement at various ages, a financial planner enables him and his new wife to feel comfortable about their prenup. The new wife can clearly see that she will be adequately taken care of and that she will have enough money to maintain her lifestyle in the event of divorce or her husband's death. At the same time, the man feels comfortable that he will be able to take care of his children, and they will have enough money to live the life that he wants them to live.

Example: A woman's main concern is that her disabled child be taken care of for life. She proposes a provision in a prenup to establish a special needs trust. Her fiancé knows how much she has sacrificed for her son and is only too happy to fund the trust.

Example: An older widow is about to remarry. Both she and her fiancé have significant assets. Her first husband had Alzheimer's and went into a home for a couple of years. She paid about $60,000 a year, so they went through a sizable chunk of assets pretty quickly. Thus, she provides in the prenup for long-term-care insurance, and she is able to remarry without trepidation.

FINANCIAL HOUSEKEEPING

A prenuptial agreement may be regarded as nothing more than prudent planning for an upcoming change in lifestyle or status. Other items that should interface with your prenuptial agreement include:

- ♥ adjusting your income tax withholding
- ♥ determining contributions to 401(k) plans, 403(b) annuities, and individual retirement accounts
- ♥ deciding upon insurance coverage: medical, dental, life, disability, long-term-care, automobile, homeowner's or renter's, umbrella, or professional liability
- ♥ selecting beneficiaries of life insurance policies; 401(k), pension, and profit-sharing plans; 403(b) annuities; and individual retirement accounts
- ♥ registering assets in individual or joint title
- ♥ writing a new will and other estate planning
- ♥ making decisions about health care for each other in a health care proxy
- ♥ stating your preference in a living will about life support
- ♥ giving the other (durable) powers of attorney in the event of incapacity
- ♥ discussing your plan with adult children and providing a copy of the prenuptial agreement to third parties

SPIRITUAL/MATERIAL WEALTH

The importance of premarital financial planning for newlyweds is more and more recognized. Financial institutions, such as Citigroup, Dreyfus, and Strong Funds, are targeting newlyweds and creating a cottage industry of premarital financial planners.

Also, financial planners are increasingly aware of

the relationship between spiritual and financial well-being.

As Mr. Calfee says: "In the medical field, they generally acknowledge that there is a strong and specific relationship between the spiritual and the scientific. If they don't allow the spiritual to enter in, the healing process is much slower."

By promoting openness and communication, prenups help bridge the gap between spiritual and material matters.

In her best-selling book *The Courage to Be Rich,* financial expert Suze Orman shows how prenuptial agreements can be enriching, both financially and spiritually:

> What I would ask you to do is unconventional: I am asking you to plan for the what-ifs while you are still totally in love. In the name of love, plan for anything and everything that could happen. Decide now how things will be split up should your feelings for each other change, and put it in writing. . . . If you have the courage to take this bold step out of love, not greed, out of wanting the best for each other, not only now but forever, regardless of what happens, then you have nothing to lose. . . . In reality, it's a way of bringing to the surface your deepest concerns about money and security and the unknowns of the future. It's not a sign of greed, weakness, or fear to want the reassurance that you both will be safe, whatever happens, and, in my experience, opening up these issues can bring partners closer together in ways they rarely comprehend until they do it.

Don't be afraid to talk about money before and during marriage. You shouldn't be embarrassed to commit your financial understanding to writing. By law, you are becoming economic partners and merging your economic histories. You have every right to protect yourself. Besides, money is integral to the marriage vow itself, which says, "For richer or poorer." Wouldn't you prefer richer, both materially *and* spiritually?

Chapter 9

SAMPLE PRENUP

&

A VALENTINE

*A*n oft-heard complaint is that the tone of a prenup is hostile and cold. Could it be, well, *more loving?*

It's a big mistake to get hung up over the language of a prenup. The document is in legalese, pure and simple. The language can't be changed very readily, because the key phrases are borrowed from statutes and case law. If you alter these phrases, it could be argued that the statutes and the case law don't apply and that something different was intended by the different wording. That's why lawyers stick with the code words. We know the judges will understand them.

Have you ever read your mortgage or lease or the regulations of your homeowners' association? These documents are in the same harsh tongue as a prenup. But they don't get in the way of hearth and home. And the language in your prenup shouldn't get in the way of love and romance.

I want to show you a *real* prenup so you will be prepared when you see a draft of yours for the first time. Your best friend probably won't want to share with you, so I have set forth excerpts from my personal prenup (with permission from my husband, of course).

Our prenup is on the simple end of the spectrum. It is suitable for a bride and groom who are each self-sufficient. (See pp. 120–126 for other possible provisions.) I've excerpted the prenup, not to deprive you of juicy details, but to spare you technical jargon. I've annotated it with a translation from the legalese and to indicate changes Bud and I made after marriage in our internuptial (or postnuptial) agreement (see chapter 16). We entered into the internuptial agreement almost six years later, in April 1996.

Our agreement complies with New York State law. Your counsel will ensure that your prenup complies with the law in your state.

Prenuptial Agreement Between Arlene G. Dubin and Bud Rosenthal

AGREEMENT dated July 31, 1990, between Arlene G. Dubin (hereinafter referred to as Ms. Dubin) and Bud Rosenthal (hereinafter referred to as Mr. Rosenthal).

In anticipation of their forthcoming marriage, the parties desire to fix by this Agreement the rights and claims that will accrue to each of them, by reason of the marriage, in the estate and property of the other during the marriage and upon his or her demise, or upon the dissolution of their marriage for any

SHUTUPS OR CONFIDENTIALITY AGREEMENTS

Your prenup generally does not need to be filed with a court to be binding. Your attorney ethically is required to keep client information confidential. If your prenup becomes part of a matrimonial proceeding, your records generally are sealed to protect confidentiality.

Nevertheless, prenups often contain confidentiality clauses. They are designed to prevent ex-spouses from talking about the terms of the agreement or the marriage.

When The Donald divorced Ivana, the parties agreed not to divulge details of their marital life, leading to a lawsuit over Ivana's novel, *For Love*

other reason. Each of the parties has a separate estate and has and expects to continue to have assets and income sufficient to remain self-supporting. Ms. Dubin has been previously married and has one child born of that marriage.

The date of the prenup is important, as it should predate the wedding by at least several weeks. Although our prenup was signed on July 31, we had both agreed to all key terms several weeks before, thus consummating the agreement well in advance of our August 19 wedding.

<u>FIRST:</u> Each party shall, during his or her lifetime, have the sole right to keep, any and all property of every kind and description which he or she now owns or may hereafter acquire

Alone. Although fiction, Donald claimed it was too close to fact and violated the shutup clause in their prenuptial agreement. Donald also had a confidentiality clause in his agreement with Marla. And Ivana had a Non-Disclosure Agreement (or NDA, as they call it in the Net Set) with Riccardo.

In that agreement, a very strict shutup clause precluded either party from discussing the marriage or the terms of its ending. When Riccardo told *The National Enquirer* that he dumped her, Ivana sued him for $15 million. She also claimed that she, not he, did the dumping.

MAZZUCCHELLI MUZZLED was the headline in the tabloids. They didn't get the scoop on whether Ivana or Riccardo was the dumpee.

---

or receive, as his or her own sole and absolute separate property, together with any income, gains, or revenues therefrom, and the absolute right at all times during the marriage, to manage, control, and dispose of the same in the same manner and to the same extent as if the marriage had not taken place and the parties had remained unmarried.

This is commonly known as a what's yours is yours, what's mine is mine waiver. Bud and I agree to retain any and all property, together with appreciation, which either one of us acquires in any manner, whether before or after the marriage.

SECOND: A. The parties further agree that, irrespective of the present or future laws of the State of New York, California, or the law of any jurisdiction other than the State of New York or California in which either party may now or hereafter have property or in which he or she may reside at any time, no property earned or acquired, whether by gift or inheritance or otherwise, before or during the marriage by either party, and none of the gains, revenues, income, appreciation in value, or proceeds from sale or exchange from and in such property, shall be marital property, community property, or quasi-community property.

This provision is basically lawyers' overkill (for the benefit of malpractice carriers). It enumerates specific instances that clarify the prior provision. Here, Bud and I reiterate our mutual waivers, specifying that they override all state laws and that they cover all property, whether earned by our individual labors or received by gifts and inheritances, and whether acquired before or after marriage, and all income, gains, revenues, and appreciation thereon and the proceeds from any sale or exchange. The waivers apply wherever we live and wherever our property is located. California is mentioned along with New York because Bud was living in both places at the time.

B. If the parties shall during the marriage acquire and hold property as joint tenants or as tenants by the entireties, then, in the event of dissolution of the marriage by reason of the death of one of the parties or otherwise, such property shall be divided in the same proportion as the parties shall have contributed to such property.

What happens in the event that Bud and I decide to hold property jointly (such as a summer home or a travel fund)? We provide that upon death or in the event of divorce, we will divide the property in the same ratio as our contributions. For example, if Bud contributed $75,000 out of $100,000 of total contributions, and I contributed $25,000, in the event of divorce, I would receive 25 percent of the value of the property.

<u>THIRD:</u> The parties hereby waive any and all rights and claims that, under the present or future laws of any jurisdiction, they may acquire upon the death of the other as surviving spouse in the other's estate or property; all rights to take in intestacy; all rights to act in any fiduciary capacity; any and all rights to receive an elective share of the other's estate; any and all rights of election to take against any Last Will and Testament of the other; and any similar rights or claims which one party may acquire upon the death of the other under the law of the State of New York, California or under the law of any jurisdiction other than the State of New York or California in which they may have property at the time of death or in which they may from time to time reside.

This is the grim reaper provision. Bud and I waive all automatic spousal rights that we would have (without this agreement) to each other's estates upon death. Such rights include the right to receive one-third of the other's estate. As indicated later in our prenup (see Fifth Article), this provision doesn't prevent Bud and me from leaving any portion or all of our estates to the other; it simply removes the obligation to do so. Several years into our marriage, Bud and I entered into an internuptial (postnuptial) agreement, providing certain amounts for each other in our wills.

<u>FOURTH:</u> Each party irrevocably waives his or her right to share in any interest of the other party in any pension, profit sharing, individual retirement plan, or similar plans. Each party shall, upon request of the other party, consent to any disposition, beneficiary designation, and selection of the form of distribution. Such consent shall be in writing, shall acknowledge the effect of the consent, shall be witnessed by a notary public, and shall otherwise be in the form required by applicable law to effectuate the foregoing.

Retirement plans can be tricky because they are governed by a technical statute, known as the Employee Retirement Income Security Act (ERISA). Here Bud and I waive automatic

spousal rights to each other's retirement plans and agree to file the consent forms which are required to be signed *after* marriage in accordance with ERISA. After marriage, Bud and I did the paperwork—a detail *you* shouldn't forget. In our internuptial (postnuptial) agreement, Bud and I amended this provision, rearranging the beneficiary designations in our retirement plans.

<u>FIFTH:</u> Nothing contained herein shall be deemed to constitute (i) a waiver by either party of any devise, bequest, or legacy that may, in the sole and absolute discretion of the other, be left to him or to her by the Last Will and Testament of the other or (ii) the waiver of rights in or to any gift made in the sole and absolute discretion by one party during his or her lifetime to the other or (iii) the waiver of rights in and to the proceeds or amounts payable under any insurance policy, pension plan, profit sharing plan, individual retirement plan, or any other similar plan under which one party, in his or her sole and absolute discretion, may cause proceeds or benefits to be made payable to the other party. Furthermore, nothing herein contained shall be deemed to preclude either of the parties from serving in any fiduciary capacity under the Last Will and Testament of the other if one party hereto, in his or her sole and absolute discretion, shall, in his or her Last Will and Testament, appoint the other party hereto to serve in such a fiduciary capacity.

We do not want to limit our largesse to each other. Bud and I may make gifts to each other, leaving all or a portion of our estates to each other, making each other the beneficiary of all or a portion of our retirement plans, and appointing each other as executors of one another's wills. The agreement eliminates the legal mandates; it does *not* bar voluntary acts.

<u>SIXTH:</u> Each party does hereby acknowledge that he or she is fully able to support himself or herself without help from the other. Accordingly, the parties each agree that, in the event of the dissolution of their marriage for any reason, neither party

shall seek alimony, support, maintenance, or counsel fees from the other, and neither party shall seek an equitable division or distribution or a distributive award out of or from the separate property of the other.

Since we are each self-sufficient, Bud and I waive any rights to receive alimony (also known as spousal support or maintenance), counsel fees, and a property settlement from the other in the event of divorce.

SEVENTH: Ms. Dubin hereby acknowledges that she has consulted Michael J. Weinberger, Esq., of the firm of Rubin Baum Levin Constant & Friedman (now RubinBaum LLP), New York, New York, with respect to all the provisions of this Agreement; and Mr. Rosenthal hereby acknowledges that he has consulted with Mel Powell, Esq., of the firm of Trope and Trope, Los Angeles, California, with respect to all the provisions of this Agreement.

Since we want to ensure that the agreement will be enforceable, Bud and I acknowledge that we each consulted with separate, independent counsel in connection with this agreement and name names.

EIGHTH: Each party confirms that he or she has received substantial financial information from the other regarding his or her assets, liabilities, and income, that each has offered to and did fully respond, directly and through his or her attorneys, to all questions the other's attorneys had concerning such financial information. Each party acknowledges that he or she regards such information as full and complete disclosure and that he or she is aware of the rights which he or she is surrendering pursuant to this Agreement. Each party hereby waives, releases, and renounces his or her right to make further discovery. Annexed hereto as Exhibit A and B are statements of the approximate net market value of the assets of Mr. Rosenthal and Ms. Dubin respectively as of June 30, 1990.

Bud and I talk turkey, something we do year-round, not just on Thanksgiving. Ensuring the enforceability of the agreement, Bud and I make full and complete disclosure of all financial matters to each other and our attorneys so that we each understand what we're waiving. We enter into this agreement voluntarily with full knowledge of the rights to which we otherwise would be entitled without an agreement.

NINTH: The parties have been advised by their respective counsel that in certain jurisdictions the spousal support and property settlement provisions of this Agreement may be invalid in whole or in part as being in violation of the public policy of such jurisdiction. In the event that a court of competent jurisdiction shall determine that any such provisions are invalid, such determination shall not invalidate any other clause, part, or provision of this Agreement.

In the unlikely event the clauses waiving spousal support and a distributive property award are held invalid, Bud and I agree that the other clauses of this agreement still remain enforceable.

TENTH: This Agreement shall be governed by the internal laws of the State of New York without giving effect to principles of conflicts of law.

New York is generally hospitable to prenups; Bud and I live in New York and are familiar with the law in New York. Thus, we agree that the law of New York shall apply to this agreement, not the law of any other state or country where our property might be located or where we choose to reside in the future.

ELEVENTH: This Agreement contains the entire understanding of the parties and may be changed, amended, or revoked only by written agreement signed and acknowledged by both of the parties. Each party shall, upon the request of the other party, execute, acknowledge, and deliver to the other party any additional instruments, and take such other action, that may be reasonably required to carry the terms and intention of this Agreement into effect.

This so-called boilerplate language belongs in almost every agreement. Bud and I have no other understanding other than this agreement and may change this agreement only by a writing acknowledged by both of us. We agree to take any actions necessary to carry out the agreement.

TWELFTH: If the parties shall agree to file any joint income tax return, each party will be responsible for so much of any tax shown as due on such return as shall be fairly allocable to the income of such party.

Bud and I are each responsible for our pro rata share of our tax liability if we file a joint income tax return.

THIRTEENTH: This Agreement shall become effective only upon the marriage of the parties to each other and shall bind the parties and their respective heirs, executors, personal representatives, administrators, successors, and assigns.

This agreement becomes effective only upon our marriage and binds our heirs.

(FOURTEENTH: Mr. Rosenthal agrees that Ms. Dubin shall not be required to do any housework or cook meals. Ms. Dubin agrees that Mr. Rosenthal shall be permitted to watch professional football on television, so long as such viewing does not exceed 35 hours per week.)

(This is an example of a "lifestyle" clause that Bud and I *didn't* include in our prenup.)

IN WITNESS WHEREOF, the parties hereto have hereunto set their hands as of the day and year first above written.

_____ _____
WITNESS   ARLENE G. DUBIN

_____ _____
WITNESS   BUD ROSENTHAL

Bud and I sign this agreement as required by law. We don't disclose the contents of our agreement to witnesses. Our witnesses *just* witness our signatures.

STATE OF NEW YORK)
)ss.:
COUNTY OF NEW YORK)

  On this 31st day of July 1990, before me came Arlene G. Dubin, to me known and known to me to be one of the persons mentioned and described in and who executed the foregoing instrument, and she duly acknowledged to me that she executed the same.

       _____
       Notary Public

STATE OF NEW YORK)
)ss.:
COUNTY OF NEW YORK)

  On this 31st day of July 1990, before me came Bud Rosenthal, to me known and known to me to be one of the persons mentioned and described in and who executed the foregoing instrument, and he duly acknowledged to me that he executed the same.

       _____
       Notary Public

Our signatures are acknowledged before a notary public, as required by New York law. [*Note: There is now a new form.*]

STATEMENT OF ASSETS AND LIABILITIES

EXHIBIT A/B

The net value of my assets as of [date] is approximately $, determined as follows:

	Approximate Market Value as of [date]
ASSETS	
Real estate (net of mortgage)	
Marketable securities	
Closely held securities	
Cash in banks, certificates of deposit, notes, etc.	
Life insurance (face value)	
Property held jointly with others	
Loans receivable	
Interests in pension plans, profit sharing plans, and other similar plans	
Interests in partnerships	
Miscellaneous assets (including but not limited to furniture, furnishings, silver, paintings, objects of art, clothing, jewelry, and personal effects).	

LIABILITIES

Credit card indebtedness

Automobile indebtedness

Student loans

Other

NET WORTH (Assets-
   Liabilities)

Annual income

Expectation of gift/
   inheritance

$$\overline{\text{Arlene G. Dubin/Bud Rosenthal}}$$

Bud and I provide full and frank line-by-line disclosure of our assets and liabilities and sign the financial statements separately.

OTHER SAMPLE PRENUP PROVISIONS

You may require something fancier than the plain vanilla prenup that Bud and I signed. The possibilities for substantive provisions are as varied as couples in the world, and the formats are as varied as lawyers in the world. There is no prescribed formula for a prenup.

I enclose some other excerpts from provisions in different prenups to give you an idea of the range of options available to you. The provisions obviously can be used for either the "Wife" or the "Husband," as applicable to your situation. I have arbitrarily used either the "Wife" or the "Husband" in my illustrations.

Your prenup must be molded to your circumstances and must comply with the specific law in your states. Clauses in the agreement must work together as an integrated whole, as any contradictions could create problems. Further, you need definitions and provisions that deal with trigger events, timing, tax consequences, general situations, and exceptional circumstances. Thus, these provisions come with a warning label: DON'T TRY THESE AT HOME WITHOUT YOUR LAWYER.

1. SEPARATE PROPERTY

The Wife's Separate Property shall include the following:

1. All property held by the Wife at the time of her marriage to the Husband.
2. All property received by the Wife during her marriage to the Husband from any individual by way of gift, devise, bequest, or inheritance.
3. All growth, gain, appreciation, or increment in the value of the Wife's Separate Property whether occurring before or during her marriage without regard to the fact that any of

the same may be attributable in whole or in part to the efforts or contributions, whether monetary or not, of the Husband.

4. All dividends, interest, rents, and other distributions received by the Wife subsequent to the marriage which shall be received by her by reason of her ownership of her Separate Property.

5. All investments and reinvestments of the Wife's Separate Property and all property received in exchange for her Separate Property.

6. All property received by the Wife as compensation for personal injuries.

The Husband agrees that he shall not have any rights in or claim an interest in or title to or possession of any Separate Property of the Wife.

In a prenup, you may list the property that remains your "Separate Property"—property that would *not* be divided in the event of a divorce.

2. DEBTS

Neither party will be responsible or obligated to pay any liability incurred by the other in his/her sole name, whether incurred before or after the marriage.

You provide that you are not responsible for your spouse's debts if they are incurred in your spouse's *sole* name.

3. PROPERTY SETTLEMENT IN THE EVENT OF DIVORCE

a. Agreement to Equally Divide Marital Property
All Marital Property shall be divided as follows:
1. One half thereof to the Husband, and
2. One half thereof to the Wife.

You agree to divide "Marital Property" evenly. Generally, "Marital Property" is property other than "Separate Property" (see Section 1 above) and covers both spouses' earnings from employment after marriage.

b. Agreement to Pay Fixed Amount

The Wife hereby promises that she shall cause the Husband to receive the sum of $100,000.

You promise a fixed dollar amount as a property settlement.

c. Graduated ("Escalator") Amount Depending on the Length of Marriage

The Husband agrees to pay the following specific amounts of money to the Wife:

Duration of Marriage	Lump Sum Payable
1 Year	$20,000
2 Years	$40,000
3 Years	$60,000
4 Years	$80,000
5 Years or More	$100,000

You agree to pay an amount that varies with the length of the marriage. It also could vary depending on annual or average income and could be capped at a maximum amount or percentage of assets.

d. Creation of Fund During Marriage—Contributions by Wealthier Party

During the marriage, the Husband shall create a fund and be responsible for putting $25,000 a year into this fund. The Husband's obligation to contribute to this fund shall continue until such time as the fund accumulates to $250,000, either through direct contribution or investment. After such time, the fund shall grow by virtue of interest or dividends earned through investment, and the monies in this fund shall be the sole and exclusive property of the Wife.

If you are the better-off party, you agree to establish a fund for the less-well-off party.

e. Creation of Fund During Marriage—Contributions by Second Wage Earner

The parties wish to establish a method to enable the Wife to save and invest all of her net earnings and for the Husband to guarantee the Wife the net amount of $20,000 per year as adjusted for cost-of-living increases. It is expected that the invested monies will allow the Wife to accumulate sufficient income-producing assets to meet her own needs in the event the marriage is terminated other than by death.

If you are the less-wealthy party, you create a net worth by saving from your own earnings.

4. Death Benefits

a. Specific Dollar Amount Bequest

The Wife agrees that upon her death she shall cause the Husband to receive from the Wife's estate the amount of $150,000.

b. Bequest of Percentage of Estate Outright

The Wife agrees that upon her death she shall cause the Husband to receive one-third (1/3) of her net estate.

c. Bequest of Percentage of Estate in Trust

The Husband shall create a trust for the Wife's benefit which will qualify for the marital deduction provided for in the Internal Revenue Code in an amount equal to one-third (1/3) of the net estate.

d. Bequest of Statutory Rights plus Additional Bequests Voluntarily Left by Will

The Wife agrees that upon her death she shall cause the Husband to receive the statutory rights of a surviving spouse provided under applicable law and any additional rights established by any valid testamentary instrument.

e. Graduated Amount ("Escalator")—Subject to a Cap—Depending on Length of Marriage

The Wife shall be entitled to receive from the Husband's estate 20 percent of his net estate, or the following amounts, whichever is less:

Duration of Marriage	Lump Sum Payable
1 year or less	$30,000
2 years or less	$60,000
3 years or less	$90,000
4 years or less	$120,000
5 years or more	$150,000

f. Marital Residence

The Husband undertakes that he shall cause the Wife to receive all of the Husband's right, title, and interest, if any, held at the time of his death in and to any residence occupied by the Husband and the Wife on a full- or part-time basis at the time of his death.

A prenup may be a contract to make a will. If you or your spouse doesn't make a will or your wills are inconsistent with your prenup, your prenup generally will prevail.

5. SPOUSAL SUPPORT, MAINTENANCE, OR ALIMONY

a. Fixed Amount; Fixed Payout Period

Commencing ____, the Husband agrees to pay the Wife $1,000 a month for a period not to exceed twenty-four months, for a maximum total payment of $24,000.

b. Fixed Amount; Indeterminate Payout Period

Commencing ____, the Husband agrees to pay the Wife the sum of $1,000 a month until the earliest of the following to occur: (i) Wife's death, (ii) Wife's remarriage, (iii) Wife's cohabitation with an unrelated male for a period of 120 consecutive days, or (iv) Husband's death.

c. Graduated ("Escalator") Amounts Depending on Length of Marriage; Fixed Payout Period

Commencing ____, the Husband agrees to pay the Wife $500 a month, for each month of the Duration of the Marriage, if the Duration of the Marriage is more than one full year, but less than three full years; or
$1,000 a month for each month of the Duration of the Marriage, up to a maximum of ten years if the Duration of the Marriage is greater than three years.

You agree to provide fixed or variable amounts for the period of time you both decide is appropriate. Spousal support may vary according to annual or average income and may be capped at an amount or percentage of assets.

6. Sunset

Upon the occurrence of the tenth anniversary of the marriage, the provisions of this Agreement automatically shall become null, void, and of no further force or effect.

You agree that your prenup automatically expires if the marriage lasts ten years.

7. Attorneys' Fees

In any proceeding to enforce the terms of this Agreement, the reasonable attorneys' fees and costs of the prevailing party shall be paid by the party who shall not prevail. If a party seeks to challenge this Agreement, the party challenging the Agreement shall pay the reasonable attorneys' fees and costs of the other party if the challenge is denied.

You agree to pay attorneys' fees and costs if you lose in a proceeding to enforce the prenup or if you challenge the prenup and the challenge is denied.

8. CONFIDENTIALITY

The parties agree that the terms of this Agreement, including, without limitation, the financial information contained herein, are and shall continue to be confidential and shall not be revealed or discussed by either one of them to or with any party.

You agree not to divulge information regarding the terms of the prenup.

9. ARBITRATION

Any controversy or claim arising out of or relating to this Agreement, or its breach, shall be settled by arbitration in accordance with the Arbitration Rules for the Interpretation of Separation Agreements of the American Arbitration Association.

You provide that any dispute arising out of your prenup shall be settled by arbitration, rather than the court system.

Chapter 10

TAKING THE COURT
OUT OF COURTSHIP

❧

FREQUENTLY ASKED QUESTIONS

he following are the most frequently asked questions I've encountered in my practice:

1. WILL A COURT ENFORCE MY PRENUP?

In the United States, courts have historically upheld prenups—in the event of death. In the event of divorce, until several decades ago, courts opposed prenups on the theory that they promoted divorce. A seminal Florida case, *Posner v. Posner,* in 1970 reversed the trend. Enforcing prenups upon divorce, *Posner* declared that public policy should not sentence "a husband and wife to a lifetime of misery as an alternative to the opprobrium of divorce."

Since then, courts in all states have generally concurred with *Posner*. The last holdout was Nebraska, where prenuptial agreements were validated in 1994. Courts today *favor* prenuptial agreements. They have noted the prevalence of divorce in American society and the adoption of no-fault divorce and principles of equitable distribution. Moreover, many courts believe that premarital agreements promote marriage, because they provide certainty in the event of divorce. Finally, in the wake of the feminist movement, courts no longer overturn prenups purely on paternalistic grounds.

2. Is there a specific statute that governs prenuptial agreements?

In 1983, the Uniform Premarital Agreement Act (the "Act") was created by a conference of commissioners in response to the growing interest in prenups. The purpose was to encourage the use of prenups by establishing a more lenient standard of enforcement. Today, the majority of states and the District of Columbia have adopted a version of the Act or statutes similar to the Act (see chart on pages 225–228).

Despite its nomenclature as a "uniform" act, the Act is *not* uniform in the adopting states. The U.S. Constitution is based on principles of *federalism:* The Constitution delegates certain powers to Congress, such as the power to declare war, while all other matters are reserved to the states, such as the authority to regulate marriage and divorce. As a result, each state has its own family and probate law and puts its imprimatur on its laws, with its unique peculiarities.

States that have not adopted the Act apply principles similar to those embodied in the Act. Some states have some form of statute regulating premarital agreements; others apply common or case law. The states that have not adopted the Act typically view prenups as contracts and uphold them if they pass muster under general principles of fairness and contract law.

3. CAN I WRITE A PRENUP THAT OVERRIDES STATE LAW?

A prenup enables you to legislate your own marriage. Within certain limits, you can write the rules and regulations that will govern your marriage. These rules and regulations generally will override otherwise applicable family and probate laws. A prenup is the ultimate libertarian dream—no need to fight city hall anymore, you *are* city hall.

If you do *not* enter into a prenup, then, like it or not, you've agreed to your state's laws, although they may lead to undesirable or inappropriate results.

A prenup is sometimes referred to as an "opting-out agreement," because you opt out of the statutory requirements of your state.

4. WHAT PROPERTY RIGHTS CAN I COVER IN MY PRENUP?

You can cover *all* forms of property. Property encompasses more than obvious *hard* assets, such as a home, jewelry, and car. It also includes *intangibles,* such as copyrights, pensions, and stock options. Business interests and professional practices, together with goodwill, are included. Some courts view an educational degree, license, career, celebrity status, or a special skill as property as well because it gives rise to "enhanced earnings capacity."

Because it is difficult to value intangibles, it is advisable to deal with them in your prenup. A party may waive his/her interest or swap it for another asset, or you and your partner can decide upon an appropriate valuation methodology.

You may specify your rights to manage and control your property. You may agree on how your property will be disposed of in the event of death or divorce and who will be the beneficiary of your life insurance policy. Finally, you may contract to make a will or trust to carry out the provisions of the prenup.

5. DO PRENUPS APPLY IN COMMUNITY PROPERTY AS WELL AS EQUITABLE DISTRIBUTION STATES?

Two systems regulate property owned by married individuals: "equitable distribution" (also called "common law") and "community property." Forty-one states, and the District of Columbia, apply equitable distribution, while nine states subscribe to the community property classification (see chart on pages 225–228.)

In equitable distribution states, the value of property is generally divided upon divorce based on a variety of equitable factors. In community property states, the value of property generally is divided equally, although not necessarily (see question 6, below). Property may be divided irrespective of who holds technical title.

Prenups are recognized in both equitable distribution and community property systems.

6. HOW WILL MY PRENUP AFFECT THE DIVISION OF PROPERTY UPON DIVORCE?

The general principle in equitable distribution states is that the value of property is divided "equitably." "Equitably" does not necessarily mean *equally*.

The court has far-ranging discretion to assign property to either you or your spouse, depending on such factors as: your income and property; length of marriage; your age and health; need of a caretaker to stay at home; any alimony award; financial and nonfinancial contributions, such as homemaking and child rearing; and tax consequences.

In community property states, although the value of community property *generally* is divided equally, courts have substantial discretion as well. Depending on the state, a judge may divide property or alter a fifty-fifty split on the basis of equitable factors, such as the nature and extent of community property and the condition in which the parties will be left by divorce. Courts also may order the reimbursement of expenses from separate property.

A judge, who prior to your case knows nothing about you or your spouse, will be randomly assigned to your case. He/she inevitably brings subjective viewpoints to bear on the decision-making process. Further, the judge will be influenced by the attorneys in your case, although they probably knew nothing about either of you prior to this case. Their personal qualities may tip the scales. To add insult to injury, this process is extremely costly, both financially and emotionally.

A prenup enables you and your partner to avoid this precarious process and agree in advance—in an atmosphere of love and generosity—on an appropriate division of assets.

7. How will my prenuptial agreement distinguish between "separate" and "marital/community" property?

A majority of the equitable distribution states and all community property states (except Washington) make a distinction by law between "separate" and "marital/community" property. In these so-called "dual property" states, only the value of marital/community property is subject to division upon divorce. You are entitled to keep your separate assets.

Such states generally provide that whatever you acquire *prior* to your marriage is considered separate property. For example, your stocks and bonds in a brokerage account you acquired before marriage generally would be considered separate. Gifts (when they are specifically intended for one person) and inheritances are commonly considered separate property—whether acquired *before* or *after* marriage.

By contrast, marital/community property generally consists of earnings from your physical or intellectual efforts *after* marriage. For example, your 401(k) account attributable to post-marriage earnings would be marital property.

A prenup generally clarifies or overrides state law, defining what will be considered separate property and what will be marital/community property in the event of divorce. You may simply list the property that you bring into the marriage, stating that you intend to keep it separate in the event the marriage terminates. You may provide that assets that would be considered separate property (e.g., an inheritance) under applicable law will be marital or that assets that would be marital (e.g., earnings during marriage) under applicable law will be separate.

In some states, no distinction is made between separate and marital/community property. These states are called "unitary" or "all-property" states. *All* property, however or whenever acquired (subject, of course, to certain exceptions), may be divided upon divorce, unless your prenuptial agreement provides otherwise (see chart on pages 225–228).

8. WHY SHOULD I BOTHER WITH A PRENUP IF THE LAW IN MY STATE AUTOMATICALLY DEFINES CERTAIN PROPERTY AS "SEPARATE"?

The distinction between separate and marital property may seem crystal clear—but it may become clouded as time goes by in your marriage.

In many states, property is *presumptively* marital/community property. This means that, if you are married, your property will be presumed to be marital/community, unless you prove otherwise. In order to show that your property is separate, you must produce books and records to trace the funds to their original separate source. This is called "tracing."

A prenup should include an inventory of assets at the time of marriage. This preserves a clear record of the assets that you bring into the marriage and becomes documentary evidence that traces your property to its separate origin.

Another problem arises from "transmutation," a legal concept that may transform separate property into marital property. For example, if you put your separate funds in joint names or if you use your individual stock portfolio to purchase a home in joint names, you may change separate property into marital property. In such cases, it may be presumed that you made a gift.

The boundary between separate and marital property also may become blurred in less obvious ways. If you mix money earned before your marriage with money earned after marriage in the same bank account, you may not be able to establish that your property is separate. This is called "commingling."

You can use your prenup to prevent separate property from becoming marital property as a result of transmutation by gift or commingling.

And a prenup can help you avoid disputes over whether *appreciation* on separate property is separate or marital/community property (see question 9, below).

9. Is the appreciation on my "separate property" considered separate property?

States arrive at differing conclusions in different contexts. Who keeps the post-marital growth, earnings, gains, rents, profits, dividends, and proceeds on separate property is often unclear in the law and thus potentially a cauldron of contention.

In some states, the determination generally depends on whether the appreciation is considered "passive" or "active." Was the property left alone or managed by a third party or did the owner actively manage it? Some states, such as Idaho, Louisiana, Texas, and Wisconsin don't abide by the active/passive dichotomy, though; others apply it only to certain assets.

Active appreciation is generally characterized as marital/community property. It occurs as a result of direct or indirect contributions—monetary or nonmonetary—of the individual spouses. The enhancement of a business as a result of your personal efforts generally would be considered active appreciation.

By contrast, passive appreciation is usually considered separate property. It occurs as a result of the efforts of others or external factors, such as random market fluctuations (e.g., inflation or interest). Examples are increases in the value of unimproved real estate, a work of art, or Treasury bills.

In a prenup, you decide for yourselves what will happen to post-marriage appreciation derived from your separate property.

For example, you may own a house and keep it in your own name after marriage with the intention that it remain your separate property in the event of divorce. The entire appreciation on the house, however, may *not* be considered your separate property if your spouse made physical improvements to it. Or if your spouse performed homemaking tasks that enabled *you* to make such improvements. A prenup can clearly state that regardless of any appreciation, the house remains entirely yours.

Similarly you may bring a stock portfolio into the marriage. The appreciation arguably could be considered marital if you actively managed it and your spouse participated in investment decisions or otherwise contributed. (Remember that hot tip he/she provided?) A prenup can provide definitively that the appreciation on such a portfolio remains separate if that's your intention.

10. WHY DO I NEED A PRENUP IF I HAVE A WILL?

In most states, your spouse is automatically entitled to certain benefits that you *cannot* reduce by a will. You can, however, agree to modify this amount in a prenup and provide a lesser or greater amount to your spouse than the law authorizes (see chapter 12).

Also, a will is a "unilateral" document, whereas a prenup is a "bilateral" document. In other words, one person creates a will, but *both* of you decide upon a prenup. Your spouse can change his or her will at any time, and he or she isn't required to inform you of any changes.

By contrast, a prenup can be changed only by mutual consent. As long as the prenup has not been revoked by both parties, its terms are enforceable against your spouse's estate, even if your spouse dies without having executed a will that conforms to the prenup.

It is, of course, advisable to execute a will that coordinates with your prenup as soon as possible after marriage.

11. CAN I SPECIFY HOW MUCH SPOUSAL SUPPORT I WILL PAY?

In general, without a prenup, the award of spousal support (a.k.a. alimony support and maintenance) is subject to the court's discretion. States have established criteria, and the courts are charged with the highly unscientific exercise of balancing the relevant factors and arriving at an appropriate dollar amount and duration. Some factors may include: income and property distribution; duration of the marriage; age and health of the parties;

PROMISES, PROMISES

Neil Simon, the world's most successful playwright, was expressly prohibited by a prenup from writing about his third wife, Dianne Lander. She didn't want him observing their relationship instead of living it.

present and future earnings capacity of each; ability of the party seeking alimony to become self-supporting, and the time and training needed to reach that point; the reduced earnings capacity due to the career building of the other party; child custody arrangements; fault of either party (depending on the state); and tax consequences. Spousal support can be awarded to either a man or a woman—each is entitled to equal protection under the law.

In general, you may avoid a subjective determination of support by agreeing to an amount in your prenup. Or you may accept a property settlement instead of support. In some states, you may provide that your separate property will not be used to pay support.

In many states, you may modify or eliminate spousal support in a prenuptial agreement to the extent that such a provision does not cause your spouse to become a public charge at the time of divorce. In some states, however, including Iowa, New Mexico, and South Dakota, the statute does *not* specifically allow modification or elimination of support in a prenup. The California Supreme Court in August 2000 upheld the right to waive support in a prenuptial agreement, although California's statute does *not* specifically provide for the modification or elimination of support.

In Indiana and Illinois, a court may order spousal support, despite its elimination or modification in a prenup, if failure to do so would cause undue hardship under circumstances that could not reasonably be foreseen at the time the prenup was signed.

12. Can I include "lifestyle" provisions?

Provisions regarding "lifestyle" issues that regulate marital behavior generally may be included in a prenup, un-

FLYING IN THE FACE OF CONVENTION

Publisher George Palmer Putnam had proposed marriage five times to the renowned aviatrix, Amelia Earhart (1897–1937), before she finally accepted. On the morning of their wedding in 1931, she handed him a letter, which is excerpted below:

Dear GP,

. . .

Please let us not interfere with each other's work or play, nor let the world see our private joys or disagreements. In this connection, I may have to keep some place where I can go to be myself now and then, for I cannot guarantee to endure at all times the confinements of even an attractive cage.

I must exact a cruel promise, and this is that you will let me go in a year if we find no happiness together.

I will try to do my best in every way.

A.E.

They were still married six years later, when her plane disappeared over the Pacific Ocean.

*From *Letters from Amelia* by Jean L. Backus. Copyright © 1982 by Jean L. Backus. Reprinted by permission of Beacon Press, Boston.

less they violate public policy or a statute imposing a criminal penalty.

These issues run the gamut from where you will live and how your children will be raised to how much Net-surfing, golf, and weight gain will be tolerated, and whether the toilet paper will unroll from the top or the bottom of the spindle.

Although there is no legal bar to the inclusion of these provisions in a prenup, you can't expect to enforce these provisions: You would be laughed out of court. The courts don't have the time or inclination to enjoin a

CONTRACTING FOR SEX
(FIVE TIMES A WEEK)

In a highly publicized sixteen-page single-spaced prenup, Rex and Teresa LeGalley of New Mexico in 1995 stated that they shall have "healthy" sex five times a week, shall always pay cash unless otherwise agreed, shall turn off lights promptly at 11:30 P.M. and awake at 6:30 A.M., shall never leave anything on the floor overnight unless they're packing, and shall never follow the car in front of them by less than one car length for every ten miles per hour they are traveling. The LeGalleys felt their prenup would solidify their marriage by discussing, analyzing, and sorting out virtually every potential conflict in advance and recording mutually acceptable solutions.

The LeGalley agreement—NOT recommended and resoundingly ridiculed—evidently worked for the couple: A few years later they reported they were still happily married.

party from smoking or to order a spouse to do the dishes. The courts don't want to meddle in an ongoing marriage.

My view is that you should enter into a dialogue, based on openness and full disclosure, about *every-thing*—both property and lifestyle issues—before your marriage. If you wish to memorialize your agreement on lifestyle issues, I suggest that you leave your prenup to cover property concerns and you address your lifestyle issues in a separate agreement (perhaps in the form of a personal letter that you lovingly sign).

Lifestyle provisions may add an aura of frivolity that possibly could prejudice a court's view of your prenup. A personal letter provides a morally persuasive statement of intent, even though it may not be enforce-able in court.

13. WHAT MATTERS MAY I NOT INCLUDE IN MY PRENUP?

A prenup cannot require you to violate public policy or conduct criminal activity. For example, a promise to smoke marijuana or an agreement prohibiting children from a previous marriage from living with you would be *verboten.* Some courts have invalidated certain provi-sions in prenups on the ground that they enable a spouse to profit from divorce—e.g., by providing an un-reasonably large sum of money if the marriage ends in a relatively short period of time. As stated in question 11, above, in many states, you may not modify or eliminate spousal support if it causes a person to become a public charge.

Your prenup may not adversely affect the right of a child to child support, child custody, or visitation. Since most states apply the "best interests of the child" standard, you—the parents—can't lower that standard.

If you include provisions relating to your children, they will constitute evidence of your intent. Courts usually consider such provisions, but they will not be binding automatically. They will be subject to judicial review and possible modification and may be voided. (But you may include—and these seem to be popular—clauses about your dogs and cats.)

In most states, you cannot limit the religious upbringing of children via a prenuptial agreement. Such a limitation is a violation of the First Amendment. New York is a notable exception as evidenced by the unholy war between Ron Perelman and Patricia Duff over whether their daughter Caleigh was being raised as an observant Jew as they agreed in their prenup.

New Mexico prohibits contracting with respect to a party's choice of abode or freedom to pursue career opportunities.

14. What financial disclosure must I make?

At the heart of a prenup is mutual disclosure of property and financial obligations. Generally, your prenup is not enforceable if the following occur:

1. you do not receive fair and reasonable disclosure; and
2. you do not waive, in writing, any right to such disclosure; and
3. you do not have an adequate knowledge of your partner's property and financial obligations.

Florida diverges from the general rule by abandoning the disclosure requirement for provisions in a

Technical Knock-Out

The heavyweight champion Evander Holyfield pointed to transcripts of an alleged telephone conversation and a letter typed by a law firm approving a prenuptial agreement with his wife, Dr. Janice. Unfortunately for Evander, at a minimum, prenups must be in writing and signed by both parties. Generally, they need to be witnessed and notarized too.

prenuptial agreement that are effective upon death (but *not* for provisions that are effective upon divorce).

The disclosure standard varies from state to state. As discussed in chapter 8, I advocate the most extensive disclosure possible—a line-by-line report of assets—in order to head off attacks on your prenup.

15. What formalities must I observe?

Generally a prenup must be in writing and signed by both parties. In some states, your signatures must be "acknowledged," which means you sign in the presence of an authorized officer, such as a notary public, who signs the prenup and authenticates your signatures. Witnesses may also be required.

As a contract, a prenup must be supported by "consideration." The only consideration generally required in a prenup is marriage. Accordingly, if the marriage ceremony does not take place, the prenup has no effect. (But a cohabitation agreement may be appropriate; see chapter 17.)

Of course, you both must be of legal age and sound mind to enter into a prenup.

16. HOW MAY I AMEND OR TERMINATE MY PRENUP?

To amend or terminate your prenup, in general, you should observe the same formalities you followed when entering the original prenup. In some states, you may have to adhere to more stringent rules (see chapter 16).

It's a good idea to provide in your prenup that it can be amended or terminated only in a prescribed manner (e.g., a signed and acknowledged writing). When you modify your prenup, it's also a good idea to recite that you intend to change or terminate the original agreement. It's *not* a good idea simply to burn the prenup.

At the time of marriage, especially if you are young, your prenup may not address certain issues, such as the birth of a child, spousal support, or the disposition of property upon death. At the appropriate time during your marriage, you may fill in the blanks by amending your prenup.

It's advisable to modify your prenup as you grow in your marriage and as circumstances materially change. In that way, you ensure the fairness and vitality of the agreement.

17. WHAT IS "VOLUNTARINESS"?

For a prenup to be valid, you must both sign "voluntarily." You should have sufficient time to consider the agreement. You need to participate in the formation and negotiation of the agreement. You should completely understand the terms and the effect of the agreement and have full knowledge of your rights upon divorce or death without a prenup. Other relevant factors for determining "voluntariness" would be your business acumen, education, and relative bargaining position. As I stated in chapter 7, the best way to show voluntariness is to consult with separate, independent counsel; fully disclose your financial affairs; and allow ample time between the prenup ceremony and the marriage ceremony.

Some attorneys certify in writing in the prenuptial agreement itself that it was entered into knowingly and voluntarily. Others videotape the prenup signing or provide a stenographic record of what was said at that time.

18. Why would a court declare a prenup "unconscionable"?

Most states focus on whether a prenuptial agreement was "unconscionable" at the time of signing the contract. "Unconscionable" means one-sided, manifestly unfair, and inequitable—in short, shocking to the conscience.

The concept of unconscionability is subject to judicial interpretation. New Jersey law provides the following definition of an unconscionable premarital agreement: an agreement which (either due to lack of property or unemployability) would render a spouse without a means of reasonable support; make a spouse a public charge; or provide a standard of living far below that which was enjoyed before the marriage.

Although many states focus on unconscionability at the time of entering into a prenup, some states, such as Connecticut and Colorado (for provisions affecting spousal support), New Jersey, and North Dakota, look at unconscionability at the time of enforcement of the contract, that is, at the time of divorce or death. In so doing, these states consider circumstances subsequent to marriage and want to know that your agreement hasn't dramatically decreased either partner's standard of living or left him/her a ward of the state.

19. Do courts care whether my agreement is fair?

Although we can't always control fairness in life, we can and should be fair in our prenups. Not only because it is the right and romantic thing to do, but also because it ensures that your prenup will hold up in court.

Fairness is an amorphous concept. Most judges determine fairness by looking at the circumstances of the parties—your ages, your stations in life, your assets, income, health, employment, your dependents, and the level of your understanding of your premarital contract.

The judgment of whether your agreement is fair may vary depending on the time frame: Do you look at fairness at the time of signing or at the time of enforcement upon divorce or death? Courts disagree. Obviously the test is more onerous if you're looking at fairness at the time of enforcement, and circumstances have changed since the prenup was originally signed.

How to beat the fairness rap? Don't be piggish. You are negotiating with your future husband or wife, after all. Don't write an agreement that provides your financially dependent spouse with nothing. A millionaire's wife shouldn't end up a pauper. Also you should update your prenup after marriage to take into consideration any changed circumstances. Besides ensuring fairness, you gain tax advantages in the gift, estate, and pension areas by transferring your property to your spouse.

20. WHAT IF MY PARTNER FORCES ME TO SIGN A PRENUP OR TRICKS ME INTO IT?

Behavior constituting fraud, deceit, misrepresentation, duress, and undue influence would render your agreement unenforceable. An example of legally indefensible behavior would be inducing your intended to sign by telling him/her that the agreement will be changed or torn up after the marriage.

A simple statement that you won't get married unless you have a prenup generally does not constitute duress. A hard bargain does not constitute duress. Duress occurs when a party has performed some act or threatened to perform some act which is wrongful in and of itself. Generally, you eliminate the possibility of these defenses if you abide by the *big three* requirements: separate and independent representation; full financial disclosure; and adequate time between the execution of the prenup and the wedding ceremony.

21. WHAT HAPPENS IF I MOVE TO ANOTHER STATE AFTER MARRIAGE?

Your prenup should be structured so that it stands on its own regardless of the state in which you or your property is located. The agreement should apply in accordance with its terms even if you move from a community property to an equitable distribution state or vice versa. If you move to another state, however, you should check with an attorney in the new locale to determine whether your prenup needs adjustment.

Cubic Zirconium Is Not Forever

In one case, a judge nullified a prenup where a wealthy car dealer deceived his wife by giving her a phony (cubic zirconium) diamond ring as an engagement ring and listed the ring as worth $21,000 on the attached financial disclosure. The wife found out a decade later it was a fake. "Fraud has clearly been proven in this case. He attempted to pull the wool over everyone's eyes, including his former wife," the judge said.

22. What is a "choice of law" provision?

Generally you may decide in a prenup which state law governs its enforceability. In today's mobile society, the "choice of law" provision is particularly important. Without a choice of law provision, a court may apply what is called "conflicts of law" analysis: It may look to the law of the state with which the marriage has the most contacts at the time of enforcement of the prenup. This could be the state where you are living at the time of the divorce, rather than the state where you were married and the prenup was signed. Usually courts will respect your choice.

If you have negotiated for the elimination of spousal support in a state that allows you to do so, you want to make sure that the provision will be enforced even if you move to a state that doesn't permit a waiver of spousal support (see question 11, above).

23. How can I discourage my spouse from challenging the prenup?

Despite media hype about attacks on prenups, most prenups are not challenged. In our litigious society, however, people commence lawsuits even with slim to no grounds. Strike suits, as they are called, also are brought to pressure the other spouse to agree to a larger settlement than specified in the prenup.

A strategy to prevent strike suits is to provide a deterrent in your prenup. You can agree that if either party unsuccessfully challenges the prenup, such party will pay the attorneys' fees and costs of the other. Or you can provide, in that case, that a portion of the property settlement will be forfeited (or increased). And you can state that if either party sues to enforce the prenup, the prevailing party will be reimbursed by the other for attorneys' fees and costs. These are called "in terrorem" measures because they threaten consequences for bad behavior.

Another approach is to provide that any disputes will be arbitrated. Compared to the court system, arbitration is a simpler and cheaper way to resolve disputes.

24. What is the time frame in which a prenup may be challenged?

Almost every civil law has a "statute of limitations." This means that you have a limited time from the occurrence of a wrong to start a lawsuit. The purpose of a statute of limitations is to provide *closure.* The idea is that you shouldn't have to worry forever that you may be sued.

Most states provide that the statute of limitations, or the period of time in which to bring an action to enforce a prenup, is suspended or "tolled" during the period of marriage. For example, if the statute of limitations is six years, you have six years from the time of commencement of a divorce action or death to contest a prenup, not six years from the time of marriage. The policy is to prevent the potentially disruptive effect of compelling litigation between spouses in an ongoing marriage.

If, on the other hand, a six-year statute is *not* tolled during the marriage, then it would be necessary to bring the lawsuit within the statutory period, whether or not divorce is contemplated. In New York, courts disagree on whether the statute of limitations is tolled during marriage, and the legislature is grappling with the issue.

25. WHAT MUST I DO TO MAINTAIN MY PRENUP?

Your actions after marriage should be consistent with the terms of the prenup. For example, if you brought brokerage accounts into the marriage and your prenup provides that they are separate property, you need to keep these in your own name and shouldn't commingle such accounts with those of your spouse. Don't put such assets into joint title.

If you don't coordinate your actions with your prenup, you will create chaos in your financial affairs. What's more, in some states, you may expose your prenup to a claim of "abandonment," that is, you did not adhere to the terms of the prenup and thus revoked it.

26. WHAT ARE THE FEDERAL INCOME TAX IMPLICATIONS OF A PROPERTY SETTLEMENT VERSUS ALIMONY?

Generally speaking, a property settlement is income tax–free to the recipient and *not* deductible by the payor. By contrast, alimony is includible in the gross income of the recipient and deductible by the payor. The rules are subject to various caveats and conditions set forth in the Internal Revenue Code. For example, spousal support must terminate upon the payee's death. Also it may not be overly front-loaded in the first three years.

You should keep these rules in mind when you are structuring your agreements and check with your adviser to assure that you have obtained the desired tax results.

CANADA: PRENUPS IN THE PROVINCES

QUEBEC

According to Karen Kear-Jodoin, domestic relations lawyer at Robinson Sheppard Shapiro in Montreal, marriage contracts are common in the Province of Quebec.

The reason, she said, is somewhat historical. Prior to 1971, if a couple did not enter into a marital contract, they would be governed by the default system of "community of property." Basically, this entailed that couples became co-owners of everything acquired during marriage, and consequently, creditors of one spouse could satisfy that spouse's debt with the assets of the other. Marriage contracts overriding this result became the norm.

In 1971, the legal regime was changed from community of property to "partnership of acquests." Under this system, generally the value of property acquired after marriage is divided equally, but creditors of one spouse cannot reach the assets of the other spouse. In 1989, the law was further changed, such that even if parties entered into a marriage contract, the value of certain types of assets must be divided equally, including family residences, furnishings, motor vehicles, and retirement plans. In addition, couples may not renounce, within a marriage contract, spousal support, compensatory allowances, custody or their obligation toward the expenses of the marriage. Because prenups are culturally ingrained—they were used by so many mothers and grandmothers of engaged couples—they remain popular.

ONTARIO

The current system generally provides for equal sharing of any and all assets acquired during the course of the marriage, triggering, at times, complex valuation issues upon marital breakdown. Couples may, by contract of marriage, contract out of the equal sharing of the value of the assets acquired during marriage, except with respect to possession (as opposed to ownership) of the marital home and custody.

The marriage contract is increasingly used in

Ontario, but Kear-Jodoin says it is still the exception, rather than the rule. She notes that while only a notarial deed is required in the Province of Quebec, the validity of a contract of marriage in the Province of Ontario may be questioned unless independent counsel has been obtained by each party.

Part Three

Do It
Your Way

Special Situations

Chapter 11

WOMEN IN LOVE

&

*A*re prenups good or bad for women?

Galen Sherwin, president of the National Organization for Women in New York, says they are a good idea. But she says that they have to be done carefully, so they help, not hurt, women.

This chapter shows how women can use prenups positively and proactively.

DO MEN HAVE THE ADVANTAGE?

According to Patricia Slatt, a New York City clinical social worker and psychotherapist: "One of the things you worry about in entering a prenup is inequality of power on an emotional level. A woman may be inclined to

HALF OF THE BREADWINNER'S LOAF

Lorna Wendt, corporate wife for thirty-one years to Gary C. Wendt, former chairman and chief executive officer of GE Capital, has become the poster woman for career wives. She argued in her highly publicized divorce action that she was entitled to half of her husband's net worth of between $45 million and $130 million, including unvested stock options. In a landmark divorce case, which called national attention to the contribution of homemakers to the success of their corporate husbands, she ultimately received something on the order of $30 million.

Ms. Wendt learned from bitter experience that all career wives should have prenups stating that they are 50 percent economic partners in their marriage. She has canvassed the country urging every woman to have a prenup before walking down the aisle. "You should know if you are a 50 percent partner or a 30 percent partner. Your marriage is going to end in either death or divorce, so you might as well be prepared."

agree in order to get married. She may have a psychological inclination to be compliant. She may naively think that the marriage will protect her."

Various theories have been put forward to explain

why women may lack leverage in negotiating prenuptial agreements. Some say that women may trade on characteristics that decline with age—such as the ability to bear children. At the same time, men may barter status and wealth, which tend to appreciate in value. Others claim that women crave intimacy and connection, while men strive for autonomy and assertiveness.

And of course, even in today's world, many women may have less economic clout than their male counterparts. They may earn less money, or anticipate earning less over time as men ascend corporate ladders while women drop down as they care for their children, parents, and/or spouse.

Thus, arguably a man can more easily walk away from the prospective marriage, giving him the advantage in the prenuptial negotiation process.

So how do you achieve both fair and loving results?

EMPOWERING WOMEN

Let's look at some modern examples of how prenups can be used to empower women:

Example: You are a fund-raiser, and your fiancé is an accountant. In a few years, you plan to leave your job to start a family. You feel strongly that your emotional and logistical support will enable your partner to thrive in his firm and that your contributions as a "nonworking" spouse and prospective mother are just as valuable as the contributions of your working spouse. You deeply believe that a good relationship favorably affects one's earning capacity as well as one's overall well-being. You want to establish up front that you are a 50 percent partner, financial and otherwise, in the upcoming marriage,

PRENUPS ADVANCE WOMEN'S RIGHTS

Traditional male-oriented divorce practices are yielding to more egalitarian practices in both Jewish and Islamic societies, and the religious prenuptial agreement has been the vehicle for this progress.

Islamic countries such as Morocco and Lebanon do not have any laws condemning polygamy, but they allow women to place provisions in a marriage contract that restrict the husband from marrying again. The woman is permitted to divorce the husband if he violates the contract.

Under traditional Jewish law, if a husband doesn't grant a wife a religious divorce or "get," the woman is considered to be in chains, linked forever to her husband—an "agunah." She may not remarry and if she has children from a subsequent marriage, they are considered "mamzarim" (bastards), who are

regardless of who is making the dinner and who is making the money. You want the security of an income stream. Accordingly, you agree with your fiancé in your prenup that all marital income will be split fifty-fifty, and all property will be split fifty-fifty upon divorce. You also agree on the amount and duration of spousal support.

Example: You work as a medical technician to support your partner through medical school. You eventually want to go to school to become a nurse practitioner. You excluded from certain privileges, including the right to marry non-"mamzarim."

In Israel and America, the religious prenuptial agreement is being used to solve the "agunah" problem. One type of agreement imposes a financial penalty on the husband for every day he refuses to grant a "get." Another provides that the marriage is annulled if the husband does not grant a "get" within a certain period of time.

In a publication of the Jewish Orthodox Feminist Alliance, summer 1999, Rivka Haut wrote: "Anyone entering a marriage today without signing a prenuptial agreement is making a major error. It's like an insurance policy; you hope you never need it, but it is good to have, just in case."

want to make sure that if you split shortly after you've made your sacrifice, you'll be able to live comfortably and further your education. You agree in your prenup that if you divorce, you will obtain a piece of your husband's medical license (i.e., a cash equivalent) as recompense for putting your career on hold. You also agree that your partner will support you through nursing school.

Example: You plan to marry a man with inherited wealth. Under the law of your state, this wealth is considered "separate" property—in other words, *his.* Most of this wealth is tied up in investments. Both you and your fiancé make decent incomes. But you and your fiancé spend pretty much every dollar you make to maintain your lifestyle. At that rate, you realize that there may be no marital property to split in the event of a divorce. Accordingly you agree to a certain lump-sum settlement in the event of divorce, irrespective of the amount of marital property.

Example: You work in New York as a physical therapist, and your clientele is substantial. Because your apartment is rent stabilized, it is considerably below market. Your fiancé just received a raise and promotion to a new job in Los Angeles. You agree to move, providing in your prenup that you will be compensated for giving up your job and apartment in the event of divorce.

Example: Your fiancé, a principal in a closely held corporation, says his family is insisting on a prenup. The family is legitimately concerned about potential discovery and valuation disputes in the event of divorce or death. You understand completely, but you don't release your interest in the business. You agree upon a settlement tied to a specific valuation formula. Obviously, if you work in the business or if your marriage lasts a long time, your share should be greater than otherwise.

The above examples show how women can redefine prenups to address their needs. In your prenup, you can clarify at the outset that you are a 50 percent partner in the marriage. If you support your spouse in his endeavors, you can stipulate the reward for your contributions. If you sacrifice your career and your educational oppor-

tunities, you can set forth the remuneration. If you both
agree that you will stay home and take care of your children, you can arrange for your compensation.

REDEFINING PRENUPS

If your inamorato wants a prenup, you should retain an
attorney (see chapter 7). You shouldn't be concerned
about antagonizing your fiancé by hiring a lawyer. It's
necessary to ensure that the agreement will be upheld.
In fact, you protect each other by hiring independent attorneys because you make the prenup less vulnerable to
attack.

Your attorney then advances your interests and
equalizes any balance of power at the bargaining table.
Your attorney will insist that certain provisions be included in the agreement for your benefit.

Other legal precautions, such as the requirement for
full disclosure, will make the process more deliberative.
The exchange of financial information will provide you
with the basis for crafting a reasonable agreement. Also,
the allowance of ample time between the prenup execution and the wedding ceremony will ensure you've had
time to reflect upon your needs. *At the end of the day,
both you and your attorney should be satisfied that the
prenup is fair.*

CLOSING THE ECONOMIC GAP

Both you and your partner should benefit in some way
from a prenup. If you are the less-well-off party, you
should gain financial security appropriate to the dura-

TRAILBLAZING PRENUP

Texan Lizzie Johnson was one of the first women to ride the Chisholm Trail. Johnson, who died in 1924, was notable for keeping her own property and making her husband sign a prenuptial agreement.

tion of your relationship, as well as an understanding and clarification of where you stand as a result of the agreement. At the same time, your fiancé should obtain appropriate protection of his assets.

When you make the revelation to one another of your net worths, you must deal with any financial disparity head on. If you are the less wealthy party, your prenup must address your financial needs. You should find a means to create a net worth or gain financial independence and security. If you work, one possibility is to allocate a significant portion of your earnings toward savings. Your husband may create a special fund for your benefit by transferring assets to such a fund over a period of time. Or he may agree to pay you a specific amount or a percentage of his net income or net worth in the event of divorce or death.

TAKE THE INITIATIVE

If a prenup is not proffered by your fiancé, you might take the first step. At the outset, state what it is you want, what you think your value is to the marriage, and what you are giving up. You should require that your husband's death or divorce will not leave you—at a minimum—worse off than before your marriage. Also, you should be compensated for your contributions—monetary and nonmonetary—to the marriage.

At the approach of marriage, you may have more leverage than you would at its exit. You probably have an independent economic base as a single woman. Your man obviously thinks that you are fascinating, since he is pledging his fealty to you forever. You are in a highly positive atmosphere, with mutual love and good feelings flowing and the inclination of *both* parties to defer to one another's reasonable concerns.

In addition, by initiating the prenup process, you might learn some things about your spouse that you didn't know before. Maybe he's not as rich or as poor as you thought. Maybe he is more generous or withholding. Maybe money is a symbol for control and autonomy, and he has a problem relinquishing it to you. You may decide to live with stinginess or egomania, but you should know about these characteristics going into the marriage. You're better off knowing sooner than later. (After negotiating a prenuptial agreement with her fiancé, one woman cracked: "I'm putting him into therapy right after the marriage.")

It's Rough to Get Justice
in the Courts

What's more, it may be a safer bet for a woman to enter into a prenup than to end up in court. You may encounter gender bias. Some judges believe they should order no more than one-third of a man's income toward the support of his ex-wife and children on the theory that the man will need the income to support his new family. In the majority of states, where equitable distribution prevails, courts are loath to award a 50 percent share to a person who earns less than her partner, especially in a relatively short-term marriage without children.

In addition, judges tend to award alimony on a temporary basis, if at all. The trend today is against awarding alimony. As an indication of its role today, it is generally no longer even *called* alimony. Rather, it's referred to as "spousal support," "maintenance," "rehabilitative alimony," or, more to the point, "short-term alimony." It's provided to give the recipient spouse time to retrain and reenter the job market. Exceptions might be made for a disabled or older spouse who has been out of the workforce and has no reasonable prospect of gainful employment.

Many judges have an overly optimistic view that the women's movement has effected a successful transformation of society. They sometimes express an unrealistic expectation that if you worked prior to marriage, you will be able to get a comparable job soon or that you can quickly convert part-time work or experience as a volunteer into a career position with a high earnings capacity.

You're in the Money

You can also use the prenup as a springboard for discussion on the more equitable apportionment of household tasks and child-rearing responsibilities, thereby freeing you to more aggressively develop income-earning skills.

Of course, today, as more women are entering and staying in the job market, a lot of you are achieving wealth and status as the "moneyed" party. You are increasingly in the position of negotiating a prenup with the "less moneyed" party. If so, you may have to apply the principles set forth in this chapter in reverse. That's the price you pay for progress!

THE KETUBAH — IN THE BEGINNING, THERE WAS A PRENUP

For about two thousand years, right down to the present day, Jews have entered into premarital contracts called Ketubot (the singular is Ketubah).

The Ketubah spells out the husband's obligation to provide his wife with food, clothing, and conjugal relations and includes the husband's guarantee to pay a certain sum upon divorce and death. The husband's promise to pay such sum is called "Mohar." The Ketubah also sets forth the dowry that the bride brings into the marriage. The dowry is provided by the bride's family and is technically leased to the groom; in the event of divorce, it is to be repaid.

According to Rabbi Allan Schranz, Sutton Place Synagogue, New York City, the Ketubah originally represented an advancement for women. The Bible doesn't mention a Ketubah. But in ancient times, women did not have any recourse if they were divorced or if their husbands died. So around the first century C.E., the Rabbis developed the Ketubah, which in Hebrew means a "written document," to protect women.

The Ketubah is considered so important that if it is lost, the woman must get a replacement Ketubah; otherwise, she is considered a concubine and is not supposed to sleep with her husband. Today, in general, the Ketubah is entered into prior to a marriage, but for most Jews it is largely ceremonial. Modern Ketubot are often artistic works that are proudly hung in homes.

ISLAMIC PRENUPTIAL AGREEMENT: THE MAHR

The "Mahr," which is part of an Islamic marriage contract, dates from the time of the Prophet Muhammad in the seventh century. Mandated by chapter 4, verse 4 of Al-Qur'aan (the Koran), it is also called "Sadaaq," which means "a token of friendship," or "Nihlah," which means a "nice gift or present." The term "dowry" is also used as a synonym.

Designed to protect women, the Mahr is a wife's right, which becomes binding upon the husband, once the marriage is contracted. It is fully payable after the consummation of marriage, but if divorce occurs before the consummation, then half is payable. The payment of the Mahr belongs to the wife only and is to be given to her only, not her parents or guardian. Only the wife can waive the payment. If the husband dies without paying the Mahr, it is an outstanding debt against his estate and must be paid before distribution of his assets to his heirs.

There is no fixed price for the Mahr in Sharee'ah, the Islamic law. According to Al-Haaj Ghazi Y. Khankan of the Islamic Center of Long Island, the Mahr could be a simple ring or even an undertaking to teach a wife Al-Qur'aan. On the other hand, the Mahr could be a sizable monetary amount, if the husband is well-to-do.

The Mahr is universal in Islamic marriages over the world. Today in the United States, it has been enforced in state courts as a prenuptial agreement as long as it is executed in accordance with the requirements of state law.

Chapter 12

MATURE LOVERS

&

Of all the special-interest groups, seniors and mature people are the most open to prenups.

The pressure is off you because you put the onus on your children. You don't want the prenup for yourself, you want it for your children.

You don't want it in the event of divorce; you want it as part of your *estate planning.*

The topic is not so ticklish. You're mature. You know what life is all about.

For seniors, the usual question is why you are getting married in the first place, not why you are getting a prenup. You answer in jest, "Because we have to." Or seriously, "Life is for the living."

Some special issues, however, arise with prenups for mature lovers.

ESTATE PLANNING

OVERRIDING AUTOMATIC DEATH BENEFITS

In general, the equitable distribution states provide that if you are a surviving spouse, you have an automatic right to a specified share of assets held at the death of your deceased spouse in his/her name. This share, to which a surviving spouse is entitled, is called a "forced share," or, more appropriately, an "elective share." The surviving spouse has the option to elect to take this share from the estate, but is not required to do so.

If your spouse didn't mention you in his/her will or gave you less than the statutory share, you would still be entitled to this prescribed statutory share. You would be able to choose or *elect* to receive an amount equal to the elective share as opposed to what your spouse provided (or didn't provide) for you in his/her will. A typical elective share would be one-third or one-half of the estate, or an interest during your lifetime in one-third or one-half of your spouse's estate. The estate would include *all* property held at death—not just "marital property" that could be divided upon divorce.

In many states, this amount of the elective share applies irrespective of the duration of the marriage, that is, whether you were married for five or fifty years. (Several states, however, have adopted a version of the Uniform Probate Code providing for a sliding scale percentage, 3 percent to 50 percent, from one year to fifteen years, based on the duration of the marriage.)

In a short-term, late-in-life remarriage, where there are children from prior marriages, the elective-share statute may provide a windfall to the surviving spouse of the remarriage who takes the elective share. In the absence of a prenup, assets from the estate can be diverted from the children of the deceased spouse to his/her stepchildren.

This *possibility* may cause your children to become antsy. They may be concerned that your spouse will receive money they would have otherwise received. "I looked after Dad after Mom died. I made all these sacrifices. Now this woman comes along," is a typical complaint.

MAKING THE TOUGH DECISIONS

In general, the law of elective-share states allows you to enter into a prenup in which you override any automatic statutory spousal death benefit. You then figure out how to leave enough money for your children while taking care of your spouse and stepchildren.

Where each partner is relatively well-off, you and your partner typically mutually waive the entire interest each of you has in the other's estate. If each of you has children, you can then each leave your entire estate to your own children.

You may decide to make certain exceptions, however. For example, you may decide to own the marital residence jointly and provide that the home goes to the survivor.

If there is a disparity in wealth, the problem is trickier. This is especially true if you both have children or have an uneven number of children. You should spell out specifically what you want in your estate plan; it's a mistake to rely on your partner's say-so that he/she will "do the right thing," no matter how trustworthy the partner.

In this situation, you may provide a greater or lesser percentage than required by law. You may agree, for example, to an "escalator" clause—a sliding-scale amount or percentage of your assets as a death benefit depending on the duration of a marriage. You may agree that, rather than an outright share, you will leave a specified amount or percentage of your assets in a trust for your spouse, and upon his/her death, to such beneficiaries as you direct.

USING A QTIP TRUST

A standard approach is to agree to set up a qualified terminable interest property trust (QTIP trust). If you die, your surviving spouse receives the income from the trust. You may also provide that the principal may be invaded for the benefit of your surviving spouse, and you may restrict distributions to specified purposes, such as the payment of medical expenses. When your surviving spouse dies, the principal of the trust passes to beneficiaries such as your children and/or stepchildren.

It may be difficult to select a trustee, who may control the possible distribution of principal from the trust. Your surviving spouse might not feel comfortable if your adult children have this power. Also the QTIP trust obviously loses its effectiveness as a planning device if a man in his seventies marries a woman in her forties, roughly the same age as his children.

There may not be a perfect solution, as you may have to pick and choose certain assets for your children and/or stepchildren and certain assets for your surviving spouse. You may also supplement your estate with the purchase of life insurance.

IN THE EVENT YOU DO NOT HAVE A WILL

In an equitable distribution state, if you do not have a will, your state probate law will dictate who will receive your property. This is called the law of "intestacy," and your surviving spouse will receive his/her "intestate" share. Generally speaking, if you don't have a will, your spouse will receive from one-third to all of the estate, depending on whether you have children or other heirs. Your surviving spouse sometimes has a right to reside in the marital residence until death. Your prenup may also override the "intestate" share statute. It is, however, generally advisable to have a will.

DISTINGUISHING COMMUNITY PROPERTY STATES

Under the community property regime, the surviving spouse generally does not need protection against disinheritance provided by an elective share in equitable distribution states. This is because the survivor already owns a one-half share of the community property. If you do not have a will, your surviving spouse will receive his/her share of the community property and in some states, also a specified share of your separate property. In community property states, a prenup can include a waiver of the surviving spouse's interest in community or separate property.

BEARING IN MIND

You may be entering into your prenup primarily to protect yourself in the event of divorce. Thus, you may feel that if your spouse is with you at your bedside (i.e., you and your spouse are still living as husband and wife) at your death, you want to leave him/her at least the elective share amount.

Prenups generally provide the *minimum* death benefit for a surviving spouse. The prenup does not prevent you from leaving *more* to your surviving spouse. Your prenup should specifically provide that you may leave more for your spouse in your will than specified in your prenup. This will prevent any claims from third party beneficiaries that a bequest is *inconsistent* with the prenup.

Since transfers to spouses are exempt from estate taxation, you must consider the tax consequences of *not* leaving your estate to your spouse.

In any event, it is always advisable to execute a will that coordinates with your prenup as soon as possible after marriage and review it in the event of the birth or adoption of a child to see if revisions are required.

Whatever you decide, you should talk to your adult children about the arrangements you have made. This may be difficult because you may not have spoken to them about these sensitive matters before. Nevertheless, you should engage in these discussions, because it will promote family harmony, make your children more accepting of your new spouse, and avoid squabbling later.

PENSION BENEFITS

Aided by the nineties boom in the stock market and self-directed 401(k) plans, retirement plans have become gigantic pools of assets. After the marital home, often they are the largest asset in the marital pot. Because of tax laws that penalize early withdrawals, retirement plan assets are unlikely to be spent. Thus, they often make a grand appearance as a sizable asset to be divided upon divorce. They need special treatment in a prenup.

Certain types of pension plans are very complicated

to bifurcate at the time of a divorce. It is difficult to determine what portion is separate and what portion is marital/community property. Often you must call in actuaries as valuation experts. Recently, some courts have divided even *post*-divorce pension increases.

As we have seen, state law generally governs family and probate matters. In the area of retirement plans, however, federal law controls. The federal law governing retirement plans is known as ERISA (Employee Retirement Income Security Act), and, because of its many technical requirements, it provides a trap for the unwary in prenuptial agreements.

Under federal law, a spouse has certain survivorship rights in "qualified" plans. Qualified plans include most company-sponsored defined benefit, profit-sharing, and 401(k) plans as well as Keogh plans for self-employed people. The IRS takes the position that spousal survivorship benefits may be waived *only* in one's capacity as spouse. If you are engaged to marry, you are *not* married. Thus, you may agree in a prenup to waive rights in a retirement plan, but you must sign appropriate waivers *after* marriage—when you have gained spouse status.

A good idea is to obtain applicable waiver forms *prior* to the marriage and attach them as exhibits to the prenup. Then you have the papers handy for signing (and notarizing) after marriage, and you don't have to start scrambling for them when you return from your honeymoon.

With respect to Individual Retirement Accounts (IRAs), you are allowed to designate any beneficiary you choose. You may designate beneficiaries other than your spouse without his/her consent. You must name your beneficiaries in the beneficiary designation forms provided by the sponsoring IRA institution. Generally, your will does not govern the disposition of IRAs. Thus, you must be careful that you update your beneficiary designations on file with the IRA institution after marriage.

If you make designations other than to your spouse, you should do some tax planning. Only spouses are entitled to tax-exempt "rollovers" of certain retirement and IRA accounts.

SOCIAL SECURITY BENEFITS

If you are divorced, generally you are entitled to a benefit commencing at age sixty-two as long as your ex-spouse qualifies for Social Security and is also over sixty-two. In addition, you must have been married for at least ten years. The benefit is the same as payable to a current spouse. The benefit is not payable if you remarry, however, while your spouse is alive.

If you are a surviving spouse, you are generally entitled to a benefit based on your deceased spouse's record if you are over sixty and unmarried (although you may remarry after age sixty without losing benefits). If you are a surviving divorced spouse, you generally are entitled to a benefit if you were married for at least ten years, are over age sixty, and remain unmarried (although you may remarry after age sixty without losing benefits).

If you remarry and forgo your Social Security benefits, you may want to provide in your prenup that your spouse will compensate you for the loss of benefits.

Long-Term-Care Insurance/Medicaid

If you do not want to deplete your children's inheritance by paying for the long-term care of your spouse (or yourself), you may want to keep your assets separate and/or purchase long-term-care insurance. Under certain circumstances, Medicaid rules allow you to decline to contribute your separate assets to your spouse's care. In addition to providing in your prenup for separation of assets, you may make provision for purchasing long-term-care insurance and payment of annual premiums.

Loss of Spousal Support

If you remarry, you may forfeit support from your ex-spouse. If so, you may want to provide in your prenup that in the event of divorce, you will be paid support at least equivalent to the amount you had received from your ex-spouse.

Naming an Executor/Trustee

You may appoint your spouse executor of your estate or trustee of a testamentary or inter vivos trust or provide that your spouse has no right to such appointment. Or you may want to provide that your spouse shall be an executor of your estate, or trustee of such a trust, but not necessarily the sole executor or sole trustee. Your prenup should make it clear if you have made any agreement as to such appointment or if you retain the flexibility to make the choice when you create your will or trust.

Naming a Conservator/Guardian

You may agree in a prenup that your spouse will not be your sole conservator or guardian in the event you become incapacitated or incompetent. Dealing with this sensitive subject protects your children if you reach a point when you can no longer act for yourself.

Similarly, in a "durable" power of attorney (that is, a power of attorney that will not be voided in the event of your incompetence or incapacity), you may designate someone other than your spouse to have your power of attorney, or you may provide that the power be shared by your spouse and someone else.

Health Insurance

You may decide in your prenup who will provide and pay for health insurance and be responsible for nonreimbursable medical, dental, prescription drug, psychiatric, and related expenses.

Health Care Proxy

You may determine in your prenup who will act as your health care agent, in the event of your incapacity, to make decisions for you regarding the provision for, and withdrawal of, medical treatment or life support measures. This agent can be a spouse, adult child, sibling, or other relative or friend.

SIGNING BONUSES:
CASH UP FRONT, NO ROYALTIES

A cash payment up front, no royalties, is a favorite device of the rich and famous. For example, Jane Fonda and Ted Turner provided in their prenup that $10 million in Turner Broadcasting stock would be bestowed on Fonda upon their marriage. In return, Jane promised not to make a claim on Ted's fortune in the event of divorce. When Turner's company merged with Time Warner, Fonda's shares were converted into Time Warner stock. After eight years of marriage, when Jane and Ted were separating, and AOL and Time Warner were coming together, Jane's Time Warner stock was estimated to be worth almost $70 million.

Chapter 13

YOUNG LOVERS

❧

"**W**hat comes to mind when you think of a prenup?" I asked some newly minted college graduates.

"Rich people," one young woman said.

"A buzz-kill," her roommate added. Elaborating for this befuddled baby boomer, she said: "If you're in love and you're marrying, it's a turnoff to sit down with a bunch of lawyers and think about unmarrying."

Her friend said thoughtfully: "I wouldn't go into a marriage thinking that I would ever get a divorce."

Another interjected, quite indignantly: "It's repulsive, actually."

You're Like a Rolling Stone

As Bob Dylan said in his popular song, "Like a Rolling Stone," "When you ain't got nothing, you got nothing to lose." This could be the theme song for young people (defined as those who are not old enough to remember the aforementioned song) when it comes to prenups.

For most, money is an abstraction. Maybe you've just begun to work for wages and pay rent; you're just about making ends meet; you haven't accumulated much to feel proprietary about. You haven't yet had your first mercenary moment, which usually occurs shortly after you receive your first big check.

It's likely that money matters less to you now than it will when you get older or when you have children. You may believe that you are marrying for love and romance and that money is not a priority. You also may believe that you are marrying your one and only true love, that your love is indestructible, and that divorce is a statistic that does not apply to *you*.

The State Pronounces You an Economic Unit

As said previously, when you sign your marriage application, you are agreeing to be bound by the family and probate laws of your state. At the very time that you are envisioning your first dance as Mr. and Mrs. or your honeymoon in Hawaii, your state is pronouncing you an economic unit, subject to the Domestic Relations Law and the Estates, Powers, and Trusts Law (EPTL) in New York (or the applicable laws in your state).

Meanwhile, it's likely that you have no idea what

these laws are. In the course of working out a prenup with your partner, you can educate yourself on the law and tailor the law to your size. A prenup gives you the opportunity to take charge of your affairs, opt out of the state system, and devise rules for your marriage that make sense to you.

You may think of a prenup as establishment, whereas actually it's counterculture, because it allows you to resist state regulation. You substitute your own private arrangement for the rules and regulations of the government. And it's not even considered civil disobedience.

You're Hot Stuff

In an intense relationship, such as a short engagement, you may not be thinking with your brain. You may feel that you are in a wonderland, where things are going so right that they can't possibly go wrong. As one young person said, "When I think back on my relationships, my emotions have overridden most logical and rational thoughts that I had in the world, in fact, almost all of them, so why not a prenup?"

In addition, your gusto and passion can lead to tremendous productivity and creativity but also may generate strife and contention. (By contrast, it is said that there would be no wars if armies were filled with senior citizens.) And, your emotional energy together with insufficient knowledge of each other and the legal system could spell trouble for your marriage.

With a prenup, you communicate with your partner and unglue the sticky issues before they gum up the marriage. You show your faith that you will not founder as a couple but will prevail. You open up to each other, identify any conflicts, resolve them, and memorialize them on a piece of paper—it's a big accomplishment. You build a foundation for a mature relationship.

Money Makes the World Go Round

Marriage inevitably involves money, and if you don't talk about finances in advance, it can bankrupt the relationship. A prenup lays the groundwork for communication about money, providing a ready-made format to uncover basic financial information about your partner. You can discuss whether you will have joint or separate bank accounts and credit cards, how you will pay down debt, how you will pay for recurring expenses, how you will handle major purchases, and how much you will save. In the course of your chat, you will also most likely reveal your economic personalities to one another (see chapter 8).

Father Knows Best

If your parents have money and have given or are thinking about giving you some of it, you will make them feel better about the marriage if you enter into a prenup. Your parents may be crazy about your choice of life mate, but they may still worry about the possibility of divorce—and the chance that *their* money could someday end up in the hands of your ex-spouse. I would *never* suggest that you do something just to please your parents, but in the case of a prenup, I feel that it is a fringe benefit. Your parents will feel more secure about the marriage and more inclined to keep those gifts coming.

Your Whole Life
Is Ahead of You

Some advisers do not advocate prenups for young people, because they feel that if you and your partner enter into the marriage without assets or dependents, you have virtually nothing to protect. In addition, they say that the future is impossible to predict, so why argue about it in advance?

The opposite is actually true.

When you're young, your entire future earning capacity lies ahead of you. You don't bring much property into the marriage—all you have is potential and prospects. Generally you split up what you acquire after marriage. Thus, if you are young, you gamble virtually all your property. You may need a prenup for clarification and protection. Do you each keep your earnings separate? Do you want to share everything fifty-fifty? Do you have some other combination in mind? What if one of you has a successful career and the other doesn't?

As for the future, you don't have to predict it, just plan for your reasonable expectations. Your prenup can be limited to matters at hand. If your circumstances or outlook changes, you can update, amend, or terminate your prenup after marriage by agreement (see chapter 16).

You Make an Educated Decision

After discussing personal and financial issues, you may decide not to enter into the prenup. You've found out about your intended's financial pluses and minuses and learned about what would happen in the event of death and divorce. You might conclude: "You know, it's not

NO BUFFOONS, JESTERS, OR SLAVES

Around 1047 C.E., Tuvia bin Khalaf, about to be married in Cairo to a young maiden named Faiza, pledged: "I will associate with proper men and not corrupt men. I will not bring into my house licentious men, buffoons, frivolous jesters, and good-for-nothings. I will not purchase for myself a slave girl as long as this Faiza is with me in marriage, except with her explicit consent." This eleventh-century document, discovered in Cairo about a hundred years ago, is an early example of a prenup.

that bad. Everything in life is a risk. I'll take the risk." But now you know what you've agreed to. You know what risk you're taking. You've gone through an exercise, and you've made a personal, conscious choice—an educated decision.

If you do enter into a prenup, you've realistically adjusted your relationship to the legal realities—your bond is economic as well as emotional. You've made a match on earth as well as in heaven.

Today, in addition to marrying later, young people are marrying less. The marriage rate has dropped. The rate per 1,000 Americans who married in 1998 was 8.3, the lowest since 1958, when 8.4 people per 1,000 were wed. As one young person said, "Either the number of prenups will increase, or the number of marriages will decrease."

Chapter 14

PARENTS OF LOVERS

℘

The issue of a prenup presents the classic challenge to a parent of an adult child: On the one hand, your child is grown up and is able to make decisions on his/her own. On the other hand, you are even more grown up and know things that could prevent your child from making a *big* mistake in the future.

If you offer your opinion, you may be considered controlling. If you don't offer your opinion, you deprive your child of the benefit of your experience and caring.

The situation is further complicated if you don't wholeheartedly embrace your child's choice of mate. Then your child may interpret any suggestion of a prenup as disapproval of his/her mate. There aren't too many issues more explosive than that. To make matters even more vexing, you know that if you don't totally approve of your future daughter- or son-in-law, the need for having a prenup is magnified.

TALK AMONG YOURSELVES

Just as the discussion of drugs, sex, and alcohol ideally should occur before your child is old enough to confront such issues, the consideration of a prenup should occur in your family prior to your children becoming of marriageable age. Whenever a high-profile divorce occurs, you can express your point of view. At that point, the discussion is held on an intellectual plane and thus could not be interpreted as a personal attack on your child's judgment. Also, the subject is in your child's consciousness, and he/she has the opportunity to present the subject to his/her partner early on in the relationship.

Presumably, if you have a family business, and your child is either a current or future owner of that business, you have impressed upon your child the importance of a prenup to the survival of the business (see chapter 15). You also have taken fallback measures—providing for buy-back provisions in the shareholders' agreement in the event of death or divorce and/or giving your children nonvoting stock.

If you haven't engaged in such talks, and the time is upon you, you might raise the subject in a gentle, nonconfrontational way or ask your child to discuss the matter with an accountant or lawyer friend of the family with whom he/she is comfortable. Or give your child a copy of this book.

As with any sensitive topic, pick a relaxed time and

a neutral setting. Explain *why* you're concerned and would like your child to pursue a prenup. Keep the focus on *your* issues. One way to do this is to use only "I" statements. ("*I'm* concerned about what would happen to the family pool business . . ." or "*I'm* afraid of having to disclose confidential material if . . .")

You May Have to Back Off

Once you've gone on record with your thoughts, keep in mind that you can't *make* your child want a prenup. And you may need to drop the conversation in the interest of a happy relationship. (Multibillionaire Ronald Perelman reportedly refused to attend the wedding of his son Joshua because he didn't have a prenuptial agreement.)

A word of caution: DON'T direct your comments to your future son- or daughter-in-law. Don't invite him or her to lunch to discuss the dire need for a prenup. The need for a prenup should emanate directly from your son or daughter, and it is his/her job to broach the topic with his/her intended. Any *interference* from *you* will likely be counterproductive. The days when parents actively negotiated premarital agreements are long gone.

Hopefully, as prenups become more prevalent, as the prenup myths are debunked, and as prenups are redefined to meet the needs of modern marrieds, your problems will lessen. There will be a buzz that prenups are the thing to do, your child's friends will be getting them, your child's partner will want one, and your child will have one. If all else fails, you can set up trusts and limited partnerships for your child's benefit rather than provide your money outright.

PARENTAL CONSENT REQUIRED

In ancient Egypt, the families of the bride and the groom were actively involved in their property settlements, since they supplied the property that the bride and groom contributed to the marriage. In one case, the prospective father-in-law required the young man to swear the following oath before a scribe: "As Amon lives, as the Ruler lives, if I should turn away to leave the daughter of Telmontu at any time, I will receive a hundred blows and be deprived of all profits that I have made with her."

The hundred blows with a stout stick, to which this groom agrees, was the same punishment meted out to convicted thieves and minor criminals.

Another solicitous father, evidently ambivalent about his daughter's upcoming marriage, promised her a place to live in the event of divorce: "You, my goodly daughter, should the Workman Baki cast you out of the house that (he) has made (for you) . . . , you shall sit in the gateway of my storehouse, that which I have made myself and no one in the land shall cast you out from there."

Chapter 15

ENTREPRENEURIAL LOVERS

&

The effect of your divorce or death on your family (or closely held) business or professional practice can be devastating. You owe it to yourself and your colleagues to minimize the destruction. An ideal way to do that is to enter into a prenup with your intended.

The reason, of course, is that a family or closely held business or professional practice is not publicly traded. It does not have a readily ascertainable market value. In order to value the business, you need to hire costly outside appraisers who require substantial disclosure to arrive at a figure. They use prescribed factors such as: the nature of the business and its history, the book value of the stock and the financial conditions of the business, the general economic outlook and the outlook for the

DON'T WASH YOUR DIRTY LAUNDRY IN HOLLYWOOD

Robert Daly, former chairman of the board of Warner Bros. (and subsequently CEO of the Los Angeles Dodgers), and Nancy, his wife of thirty years, were going through a contentious divorce, sans a prenup. Bob, under pressure from Nancy's lawyers, had to reveal the details of his lucrative long-term incentive plan, valued at $31 million, plus his options on almost three million stock shares of Time Warner, the parent company.

What probably pushed the financial matters toward an out-of-court settlement was the threat of Nancy's lawyers to force testimony from other Time Warner executives. The lawyers moved to depose Bob's co-chairman, Terry Semel, and Gerald Levin, top executive of Time Warner, who was ultimately responsible for both their contracts. By settling (for an estimated $45 million), Bob avoided the embarrassment of having Levin and Semel, his boss and colleague, testify publicly about the intimate details of their compensation.

specific industry, the earnings capacity of the business, dividend-paying capacity, the "goodwill" value, the market price of similar companies, sales of stock, and the size of the block of stock to be valued. The *date* of the valuation—whether at the commencement of a matrimonial action or the time of trial—also can be a controversial issue.

Even a relatively straightforward appraisal can be a nightmare for you and your company.

During divorce or estate litigation, a protracted discovery period may be disruptive to your business and may force you to divulge information you would prefer to keep private. In addition, you will pay a fortune in accounting and legal fees.

YOUR BUSINESS IS YOUR
SPOUSE'S BUSINESS

In general, the value of your interest in a business is considered "marital property," subject to division upon termination of a marriage. Your business is built by the grease of your elbows; such labors are your contributions to the economic well-being of the marital partnership and thus classic marital property.

Even if you started your business prior to marriage in a state that considers such business "separate property," the appreciation in value of such business and/or the income therefrom generally is considered marital property. Your spouse may have made indirect contributions to the business as a homemaker or hostess. And if your spouse worked in the business, particularly for no or below-market compensation, he/she would be entitled to an even greater share.

Accordingly, you may provide in your prenup that your partner waives his/her interest in your business in

BRUISING BUSINESS BREAKUP

Ronald Meyer, co-founder of the privately held Creative Artists Agency and later head of Universal Pictures, endured a divorce in 1989. His wife, Ellen, demanded a share of Ronald's 22 percent interest in CAA. The judge ordered CAA to open its books so a valuation could be performed. The case was settled out of court shortly thereafter.

exchange for your reciprocal waiver of an interest in your partner's assets. Or your partner may waive any interest in your business in exchange for an agreed-upon sum of cash or specific items of property, such as the marital residence. If you do agree that your spouse should receive a stated percentage of your business, you should clearly state a specific valuation formula. The formula should be the same as that provided for in any shareholders' or partnership agreement. That way, at the very least, you remove the methodology from contention.

Example: A woman and her fiancé plan to launch their own separate businesses. Each has business partners and feels a duty to them to avoid messy valuation litigation. Accordingly they sign a prenup waiving any interest in the other's business in the event of divorce.

In four years, the wife's business fails while the husband's business flourishes. The wife becomes the prime caretaker for their children, while working part-time in her husband's business. They modify their prenup to provide that in the event of divorce, the wife would be entitled to half the value of the business. They agree upon a specific valuation formula, with the concurrence of the husband's business partners, and a cash payout in installments.

Example: A couple of cooks start a restaurant together. They agree in a prenup that if they ever divorce, one would buy the other out of the restaurant. They figure out in advance their price methodology—a "Scotch auction": one spouse names the price, and the other has the option to buy or sell. This prevents an all-out battle as to the ultimate ownership and valuation of the business. And it prevents the business from becoming a divorce battleground. They celebrate the prenup with a bottle of Scotch and Scotch salmon.

THERE'S NO BUSINESS LIKE THE FAMILY BUSINESS

Generally the goal is to ensure that your ex-spouse or the estate of your deceased spouse will not become an owner of your business. If that occurs, the ownership may fall out of friendly or capable hands. Along the same lines, hopefully your child has his/her prenup or internup in place if you are transferring stock in the family business to him/her.

If you work in a business, you should provide in your prenup that your partner agrees that your salary represents fair market value compensation for your services. Otherwise, in the event of divorce, your spouse

AN EDUCATED CONSUMER

Marcy Syms, who runs her father's off-price clothing chain, Syms Clothing Store, based in Secaucus, New Jersey, readily signed a prenuptial agreement. She said: "Of course you must love each other and think you'll be together forever, but what you're really doing is combining estates. In case of divorce, you don't want to destroy your family business over a personal failing."

could argue that you were in fact being compensated in the form of stock, and he/she is thus entitled to a portion of such stock.

Fifty percent of all businesses are family owned. There are roughly 13 million family businesses in the United States. In the next fifty years, between $40 and $136 trillion in wealth will change hands. Much of this consists of stock ownership in family businesses. If one of these businesses is yours, you owe it to yourself and your children to keep the tradition alive.

Chapter 16

INTERNUPS

❧

JUST BETWEEN US MARRIED FOLK

Often when I bring up the topic of prenuptial agreements to married folk, they joke: "Is it too late for me?" I cause a little stir when I reply: "No, it is not. You can have a postnup, a midnup, or an internup, and more and more people are doing them."

Postnuptial, midnuptial, or internuptial agreements refer to agreements between spouses. They are similar to prenups except they are signed *during* a marriage. They are not separation agreements, because they are *not* signed in contemplation of a separation or a divorce. Rather, they are designed to protect and further an ongoing, viable marriage. That's why I prefer the term internuptial agreement, or internup, because "inter" means "during." Also, the word *internup* conjures up "interplay," "interact," and, of course, "intercourse."

As internups become better known, they are being used more. You may enter into an internup if you didn't get around to signing a prenup before you were married. Perhaps you didn't think of a prenup, you were afraid to bring it up, or you didn't need an agreement *then,* but *now* your situation has changed. You may enter into an internup if you and your partner signed a prenup, but now you want to alter the terms of the original prenup. A prenup that is amended after marriage is an internup.

Donald Trump's prenuptial agreement with Ivana was entered into in 1977 and updated *three* times during their marriage, which ended in 1990. Ivana thus demonstrated her assent to the terms of the contract in the light of the changed circumstances of their marriage (i.e., The Donald's ever-growing fortune).

WHY YOU MAY BE INTERESTED IN AN INTERNUP

You might be interested in doing one if you have inherited some money, received some stock options, or sold your business. You may be leaving your job to stay home with the children and want to spell out your compensation for your noneconomic contributions to the marriage. You may have suffered reverses in business or incurred a disability and want to ensure a means of support in the event of divorce or death of your spouse.

You may use an internup to cover the spectrum of

issues generally covered in a prenup or to address one particular problem.

Example: A couple has been married for ten years, but recently their relationship has been strained. The husband has four children from a previous marriage, while the wife has two children from a previous marriage. The wife has only a distant relationship with the husband's four children, who were young adults at the time she married their father. A few years ago, the wife received a substantial inheritance from her parents, which she wants to bequeath to her two natural children. In order to put the wife at ease, the husband and wife sign an internuptial agreement, whereby the husband waives his right to receive any portion of the wife's inheritance upon her death.

Example: A couple marry at a time when the groom has a successful advertising business and a net worth of about $500,000. In their prenup, he agrees to pay his bride a certain amount each year, up to a maximum of fifteen years, if they divorce. In the fifth year of marriage, the husband sells his business for $50 million. He and his wife enter into an internup substantially adjusting the annual sums.

Example: One of three optometrists in private practice recently was divorced. The practice was subject to extensive and embarrassing discovery by the optometrist-partner's ex-wife. Questions arose such as what percentage of automobile and telephone expenses was for business versus personal use. Now the other two optometrists are concerned about each other's marriages. They don't want to go through a similar ordeal again.

They agree to engage in the internuptial process with their wives.

Example: A wife discovers her husband is having an affair. The wife tells the husband she wants a divorce. The husband insists that the affair is over, it didn't mean anything, and he doesn't want a divorce. The wife is skeptical. The husband shows his sincerity by entering into an internup with his wife, providing very favorable terms. The couple remains married.

Example: A wife manages real estate properties. The husband is a travel agent who recently inherited $2 million. The husband urges the wife to quit her job so they can spend more time together, especially on overseas travel. The wife has been the family's primary wage earner and financial planner. She asks her husband to put the inheritance in joint names so they can share control over investment and budgeting. Also, she preserves her claim to the inheritance in the event of divorce. They memorialize their understanding in an internuptial agreement and happily plan their first trip to Belize.

REDUCE STRESS

An internup can ease tension over property matters. Often such an agreement will "wall off" certain property and designate it as the separate property of one spouse. Such property becomes "off limits" to the other spouse in the event of a divorce or death. Or you may use your internup to transfer wealth or to share your good fortune with your spouse. For example, you may agree to add your spouse as co-owner of the beach cottage you brought into the marriage or purchased with an inheritance. Now who said internups aren't romantic?

An internup can be very effective if you or your spouse have an emotional need for security. For example, a spouse with little property in his or her name may not be satisfied with the promise that "everything is under control." In an internup, you disclose your assets and liabilities and gain assurances about what will happen in the event of your spouse's death or divorce.

After you have been married for a while, you may learn more about each other and may do some planning that you haven't done before. For example, you may come to realize that you know how to save and invest your money, while your partner is more freewheeling. You may feel that your spouse is wasting money that you want to pass down to your children. As much as you love your spouse, you want an internup to protect your children.

You also can use an internup for reconciliation purposes. For example, if you have had marital difficulties, you may decide to kiss and make up, using your internup as a security blanket.

Just like a prenup, an internup can be a catalyst for communication with your spouse or provide a mechanism for resolution of disputes. By working out your problems and putting them behind you, the problem no longer festers. Your marriage is stronger as a result.

YOU MAY ALREADY HAVE ONE

You might have an internup without realizing it. You may have agreed to transfer some property to your spouse, and you may have put your property in your spouse's name pursuant to your understanding. Once you do, you can't undo—unless your spouse agrees. For example, if you previously owned a cottage in your name and you transfer it to your spouse, as a practical matter, your transfer is as binding as if you entered into an internuptial agreement.

An internup may be viewed as not something new, but as a refinement of a widely accepted practice—interspousal property transfers. (Such interspousal transfers are fairly common among older couples who make them for estate planning purposes.)

THE SAME, BUT DIFFERENT

Unlike prenups, there is no uniform act that applies to internups. The Uniform Premarital Agreement Act (the "Act") applies specifically to prenups only (see chapter 10, question 2). Colorado, which has modeled its law after the Act, specifically applies the law to both prenups and internups. Most other states recognize internups either explicitly by statutes allowing married persons to contract with each other, implicitly through statutes regulating certain terms or requiring recording of such agreements, or as a matter of "case" or "common" law.

The general rule in this emerging area is to apply the same rules for internups as for prenups. In some states, though, internups and prenups are subject to different procedural and substantive requirements. As with prenups, it's best to have representation by separate, independent counsel, who will advise you of any such distinctions.

For example, in certain states, oral internups may be

valid, whereas others specifically require them to be in writing. (Although oral internups may technically be enforceable, remember that "pillow talk" is very hard to prove!)

In Louisiana, a couple must jointly petition a court to approve an internup, and the court must find it in the couple's "best interests." In Minnesota, an internup is allowed only if it complies with the requirements for a prenup and at the time of execution of the internup, each spouse is represented by separate counsel; each has a net worth of over $1.2 million; and the couple stays married for two years after signing.

THEY ARE SOMETIMES HELD TO A HIGHER STANDARD

Some courts scrutinize internups more carefully than prenups, sometimes holding internups to a higher standard of fairness on the theory that the parties have less leverage in internups than in prenups.

Prior to marriage, both parties are on the brink of changing their lifestyle. They have a choice of remaining in their current stable single state or embarking on a new way of life. After marriage, however, their choices are more difficult. One party may take unfair advantage of his/her spouse's vulnerability—his/her reluctance to divorce in order to avoid the destruction of the family, change in social status, and other consequences of divorce.

For example, a New Jersey court overturned an internup that the wife signed, against advice of counsel, after her husband threatened divorce, "unheard of" in her family. He said he would not pay support and the wife and her sons "would live in a little shack and the kids would go to public school."

In a Florida case, a court invalidated an internup where the husband threatened the wife that "she had better find a lawyer who would let her sign the agreement or he would blow up the house and throw Clorox all over her clothes."

A few courts take the position that internups promote divorce or that they are coercive to women, who, according to these courts, have more to lose once they are married. As a result, they have invalidated agreements upon a finding that one spouse took advantage of the other's efforts to save a stormy marriage, badgered a spouse into signing, or took unfair advantage of a spouse's disability.

But in general, most courts believe that properly executed internups promote domestic harmony, reduce probate problems, and lessen the intensity of any divorce proceeding.

Bringing Up the "I" Word

Raising the subject of an internup may be just as sensitive as bringing up the topic of a prenup (see chapter 5).

It obviously helps if you and your partner entered into a prenup. Then the internup is a natural extension of the prenuptial process. Some couples periodically review and update their prenup, even arranging regular romantic getaways to do so. Other couples realize the need to amend their prenup when their circumstances change, for example, if a child is born or adopted, or if they experience a significant economic up- or downturn.

If you have not entered into a prenup, proceed as delicately as possible. As with a prenup, you should approach the topic from a collaborative viewpoint. You should state your concerns in a straightforward fashion at the same time as you solicit your spouse's input and feedback. As with a prenup, you must remain open-minded and prepared to make compromises in the negotiation.

You can use the occurrence of a change in circumstance as the appropriate time to bring up an internup. You might segue into the topic when you discuss children or retirement. Also, you can present this book as a starting point for conversation. Perhaps your attorney or financial planner will raise the issue in conjunction with your overall financial planning (see chapter 8).

When you're doing your wills and your other estate planning documents, you also can do your internup. The internup is just one more document to enable you to avoid disagreements and costly litigation.

Chapter 17

QUASI-NUPS

☙

COHABS AND PRE-PRENUPS

A big fuss is often made about the rising divorce rate in America in the last several decades. The rate doubled from 1960 to 1990. At the same time another equally telling statistic is often ignored: the falling marriage rate. It has dipped to its lowest level in four decades. The number of U.S. households consisting of two unrelated adults increased from 2.8 million in 1980 to nearly 6 million (4.1 million unmarried couples of the opposite sex and 1.8 million couples of the same sex) in 1998. And the number is likely to rise, since living together is becoming an acceptable lifestyle that no longer carries a social stigma.

The statistics reflect a number of different categories of cohabitants:

♥ same-sex couples who can't legally marry
♥ young people who live together to reduce expenses
♥ older people who either don't want to upset their children or want to maximize their government benefits

As discussed in this book, most people who remain in an unmarried relationship can use a prenup as an enabler—to overcome the barriers to marriage. In the case of many unmarrieds, you may feel you have a prenup in fact, although not in law (a "de facto" prenup). You are in a committed emotional relationship, but you have separate financial lives. Each of you owns your property separately without any sharing with the other upon death or divorce. You thus avoid commitment and complications, legalisms, and logistics.

But are you truly getting what you want? Although you regard your partner as a family member, the law may *not* take care of your partner in the manner in which you intend. Paradoxically, the law may provide benefits for your partner in a manner that you do *not* intend.

You Are Strangers in the Eyes of the Law

In many states, unless you have a cohabitation, living-together, or interpersonal agreement (a "cohab"), in the event of death or breakup you and your partner will be treated as legal strangers. If you don't take affirmative steps (such as providing for your partner in a will, designating your partner as the beneficiary of your life insurance plan or retirement plan, or titling your residence as joint tenancy with right of survival), you will not share in one another's property. For example, if you die without a will, your property, including your home, generally will pass to your next-of-kin—your blood relatives—not your partner.

Thus, if you want to share with your partner, you need a cohab even more than engaged couples need a prenup. The law provides a default system of protection for marrieds. It may not be the optimal system, but nevertheless a system is in place. *With respect to unmarrieds, there is no safety net at all.*

Married couples, simply by virtue of their relationship, accrue certain legal rights, such as the right to receive a property settlement and/or support in the event of divorce; file joint tax returns; receive distributions from estates free of estate tax; receive survivor's benefits from retirement plans and Social Security; obtain "family" health insurance, dental insurance, bereavement leave, and other employment benefits; and automatically share in his/her partner's property in the event he/she dies without a will.

Such rights reflect the states' recognition of marriage as a lasting partnership as well as the government's interest in promoting marriage, preventing divorce, and ensuring the financial stability of former spouses and minors upon divorce. These rights do not generally inure to the benefit of cohabitants, who must take express action to secure benefits. *You have to create your own benefits and rights for you and your partner in a cohab.*

Some private employers offer employment benefits to "domestic partners." In some cities, and in the state of California, you may register as domestic partners. In general, registration entitles you to limited benefits offered by participating employers and some rights under local law. On July 1, 2000, Vermont became the first in the nation to establish a "civil union" as the same-sex counterpart to marriage in the state (see page 213).

YOUR PARTNER IS YOUR PAL
(AS IN "PALIMONY")

At the same time that many states exclude cohabitants from the range of legal protections available to married people, other states take it upon themselves to confer rights on cohabitants, applying a theory known as "implied-in-fact" contract (see table on pages 229–233). An implied-in-fact contract is one that is implied from your course of behavior and the circumstances of your relationship. If you think that definition is unclear, the courts agree with you. Depending on the particular jurist in the particular jurisdiction, you get a different conclusion. Because of the nebulous nature of the concept, it is difficult, frustrating, and expensive to prove or disprove the existence of an implied-in-fact contract.

For example, in some states, if you jointly contribute to the cost of purchases, you may be presumed to intend to split property in the event of dissolution of the relationship. If you jointly operate a business and spend your own money on supplies and equipment, upon breakup you may be entitled to one-half of the appreciation and reimbursement of the items you purchased. If you give up your career to move in with your significant other to become a full-time homemaker and parent, you may be entitled to be compensated for those labors in the form of support or otherwise. If you live together and pool your assets and earnings, you may be entitled to share income from your joint labors.

DECIDING UPON THE MERITS

In addition to an implied-in-fact theory, some state courts use other equitable doctrines to apportion assets between cohabitants to prevent hardship and injustice, as they see it. These doctrines include agreement of partnership, joint venture, "quantum meruit," "unjust enrichment," and "constructive trusts." Quantum meruit refers to a claim based on the reasonable value of services. Unjust enrichment refers to the retention of a benefit conferred, without offering compensation, in circumstances where compensation is reasonably expected. A constructive trust is a trust imposed against someone who has obtained property by wrongdoing.

Other courts reject these theories on public policy grounds. Either they believe that the application of such theories amounts to a judicial creation of common law marriage, or they believe that to equate cohabitation with marriage would violate state marriage laws, which are designed to promote marriage. Finally, to quote one court, they believe that they "run great risk of error to attempt through hindsight to sort out the intentions of the parties and affix jural significance to conduct carried out within an essentially private and generally noncontractual relationship."

DOES YOUR PARTNER'S SEX MATTER?

The public policy ground against implied-in-fact cohabitation contracts is more often invoked in the same-sex than heterosexual context, although the distinction is less pronounced than in the past. For example, in a 1997 case, a Florida Supreme Court found that an implied contract for financial support between two female cohabitants did not violate public policy. Florida law, however, expressly prohibits adoptions by gays and same-sex marriages. Moreover, Florida recently enacted a law that prohibits legal recognition of same-sex marriages, regardless of whether such marriages were formed validly in another state.

Many states besides Florida have enacted or proposed similar legislation as a result of the Defense of Marriage Act (DOMA), which was passed by Congress in 1996. DOMA is a federal statute that refuses to recognize same-sex marriages for entitlement to federal benefits. It also specifically allows states to refuse to recognize same-sex marriages formed in other states. At this writing, Vermont recognizes same-sex marriages in the form of "civil unions," and successful challenges have been mounted against laws that prohibit same-sex marriages in Hawaii. The constitutionality of DOMA and related state statutes has not yet been determined.

Write Your Own Ticket

The way to protect yourself and your mate against a morass of vague and inconsistent rulings is to enter into an express cohabitation agreement, which clarifies your rights, obligations, and understandings. Although Georgia, Illinois, and Louisiana prohibit express cohabitation agreements, virtually every other jurisdiction enforces them. Furthermore, while some states still have statutes banning unmarried cohabitation, most of these will nevertheless enforce property rights of cohabitants.

A cohabitation agreement is a private contract between the parties. Technically you can enter into either an oral or written contract, but don't even think about an oral contract, because it's extremely difficult to prove. You're basically in a situation of "He said/She said," or "He said/He said" or "She said/She said." At a *minimum,* you would need a reliable corroborating witness. And some states hold that the "statute of frauds," which requires a signed writing to prevent fraud and perjury, applies to cohabitation agreements.

When entering into a cohab, one option is to follow the procedural rules that are applicable to prenups, although not legally required. Since these rules are generally stricter than general contract principles, and since they apply to a similar subject matter, you will be on safe ground in your cohab if you adhere to the higher standard of the prenup. Key procedural rules would be retaining separate and independent counsel and making full and fair disclosure.

CLEAN UP YOUR ACT

As stated, you need a cohab to avoid a legal vacuum. In addition, you may need a cohab to avoid being swept up in a dust storm of implied-in-fact contracts and other equitable doctrines. Other reasons for entering into a cohab are much the same as for entering into a prenup: to guarantee the financially less secure partner an equitable settlement in the event it becomes necessary to divide assets; to properly compensate a party for spending years as a homemaker; to allow the financially more secure party to limit exposure in the event of a breakup; to clarify your rights and obligations; to disclose your expectations of the relationship, both financial and personal; and to address these issues at a time when you are loving, level-headed, and favorably disposed toward one other, not when you're in the throes of a messy split, when you're feeling hurt, angry, and uncommunicative.

The emotional resistance to a cohab of course can be the same as to a prenup: Your partner may infer a lack of trust or commitment to the relationship. Of course, logically the opposite is usually the case. An uncommitted cohabitant without a contract often can walk out without sharing anything; a committed cohabitant with a contract usually agrees to provide for his/her partner upon dissolution of the relationship.

It's Not Just for Sex

Prior to 1976, courts across the country routinely voided cohabs as being contrary to public policy: They were considered contracts for "meretricious sexual services" or prostitution. In that year, the California Supreme Court in a landmark case, *Marvin v. Marvin,* rendered a sweeping decision in favor of Michelle Triola Marvin, who claimed that she gave up her career as a dancer to be a full-time homemaker and companion in exchange for the late actor Lee Marvin's oral promise of lifetime support. The court declared that the "fact that a man and a woman live together without marriage, and engage in a sexual relationship, does not itself invalidate agreements between them" and authorized express and implied agreements and other equitable remedies.

Today, as long as sex is not the sole consideration for the contract, you can agree upon virtually anything. It's okay to say in the cohab that you'll be a homemaker or housekeeper for your partner in some states—as long as you don't say *lover.* Otherwise, a cohab is a very flexible laissez faire document, less subject to regulation than a prenup. For example, you can waive financial support in a cohabitation agreement, whereas in certain states you are not permitted by law to do so in a prenup (see chapter 10, question 11).

A cohab typically tries to establish contractually for the parties the rights and obligations that married people obtain by custom, statute, and agreement.

ALL SIZES AND SHAPES

Like prenups, cohabs come in all sizes and shapes. You can agree to keep all property separate, to share all property, to share ownership only of a specific jointly acquired item, to support your partner while he/she goes to school, or to compensate your partner for giving up his/her career to be a homemaker/childcare giver.

If you live in a state that recognizes common law marriages (see table on pages 229–233), you should include a provision making it clear that you and your partner do not intend to form a common law marriage.

You can also include lifestyle provisions such as how the children will be raised, how the household duties will be divided, and who will take the dog out for a walk. It is not advisable to include provisions about sexual relations because of the legal sensitivity in this area. Lifestyle clauses in cohabs, as in prenups, serve as "reminders" and are not generally enforceable in court.

In conjunction with cohabs, unmarrieds should consider registering their real property as joint tenants with a right of survivorship. This ensures that your home will revert to your partner automatically upon death. In the event of a breakup, the property will be partitioned. In addition, unmarrieds should take special pains to name each other as beneficiaries in their wills, retirement

WHAT TO COVER IN A COHAB

In a cohab, you typically cover the following key points:

- ♥ distribution of property upon breakup of the relationship
- ♥ obligation to contribute to the support of the household or, upon dissolution of the relationship, to pay financial support
- ♥ payment of debts
- ♥ disposition of marital residence upon breakup of the relationship
- ♥ support, custody, or visitation rights for minor children (although nonbinding)
- ♥ surviving party's right to inherit property and receive pension benefits, life insurance, and other entitlements
- ♥ health insurance
- ♥ right to serve as guardian/conservator in the event of incapacitation
- ♥ right to make medical decisions

plans, insurance policies, health care proxies, and powers of attorney. No automatic protection arises in the event of an oversight, as is the case with marrieds. You may also require special planning in the estate and retirement areas to compensate for the lack of special benefits that are available to spousal beneficiaries.

A Cohab Is Not a Prenup

As we have seen, a cohab is quite different from a prenup. Don't make the mistake of confusing them. A cohab will *not* have the same force and effect *after* marriage as a prenup. Because of the states' interest in promoting marriage, most states have adopted legislation prescribing specific requirements for prenups (see chapter 10, question 2). In contrast, very few states have adopted laws to deal with cohabs, and they are governed almost exclusively by general contract principles. In addition, while a prenup goes into effect only upon marriage, a cohab usually isn't valid once the parties marry.

Are You Single or Married? (This is Not a Trick Question)

The difference between cohabitation and common law marriage is *critical*. They are *not* synonymous. Only certain states recognize a common law marriage, and cohabitation itself does not constitute a common law marriage. If you are a cohabitant, you are legally considered single; if you are common law married, you are legally considered married to the same degree as if you had a ceremony.

The District of Columbia and eleven states recognize common law marriage: Alabama, Colorado, Iowa, Kansas, Montana, Oklahoma, Pennsylvania, Rhode Island, South Carolina, Texas, and Utah. Two states, New Hampshire and Oregon, recognize common law marriage only at death. Oregon requires a cohabitation period of ten years, while New Hampshire specifies three years, immediately prior to death.

How do you qualify for a common law marriage in these jurisdictions? You and your partner must agree in writing or orally to enter into a husband/wife relationship. Most of these jurisdictions also require you to hold yourselves out as husband and wife and acquire a reputation as a married couple.

Many states that do not recognize a common law marriage formed within their borders will nonetheless recognize a common law marriage validly created in another state. For example, although Tennessee does not recognize a common law marriage established there, it will recognize a common law marriage validly entered into in Alabama. Once the marriage is recognized as a common law marriage, it is treated no differently than a ceremonial marriage, for example, entitling the surviving spouse to receive statutory benefits or a certain share of the deceased spouse's estate.

Some states, such as Arkansas, Illinois, and Minnesota, refuse to recognize common law marriages among their residents even if such marriages were validly formed under the laws of other states.

You must *intend* to create a common law marriage. If there is evidence that you or your partner has stated that you aren't married but are just living together, you could destroy a claim to common law marriage.

ARE YOU READY FOR A PRE-PRENUP?

If the idea of some court determining your marital status makes you uneasy, and you want to make sure that your cohabitation doesn't unwittingly become a common law marriage, you may be a candidate for a pre-prenup. The following is the substance of an affidavit that one couple used, but as with any form, it must be custom-tailored to your situation by an attorney who applies the law in your state. Also, as with any agreement, your actions must be consistent with it.

We, _____, and _____, both over 21 years of age, hereby affirm and state that I, _____, and I, _____, are not married as of this date, that we are not living together as man and wife, and that we have not represented to others that we are married. We further say that if we do marry, we will obtain a marriage license and enter into a ceremonial marriage.

This Affidavit and Agreement is executed so that both parties confirm that there has not been and there will not be an informal marriage between themselves and if they desire to be married, they will do so in a ceremonial marriage with a marriage license issued from the appropriate state.

Both parties waive their rights, if any, to receive maintenance, support, or any other payment from the other. Neither party will incur any debts or obligations for which the other will be responsible without the prior written authorization from the other party.

This Affidavit and Agreement applies as long as the parties do not enter into a ceremonial marriage with a marriage license.

Both parties have read this Affidavit and Agreement voluntarily and freely and without any coercion, duress, or undue influence from the other.

LIGHTER MOMENTS

⊗

HAVE I TOLD YOU LATELY THAT YOU
HAVE BEAUTIFUL PRENUPS?

It's my fond hope that after reading this book, you no longer think that prenups are about gaining leverage over your partner or vice versa. Now maybe you're ready to consider the levity of prenups. Throughout this book, I have stressed the importance of communication and openness in your relationship. High up there in importance also is a sense of humor. So, in closing, I would like to share with you a few examples of the lighter side of prenups.

LOVE MEANS NOTHING
TO A TENNIS PLAYER

In 1997, Marylou Whitney, seventy-one, socialite and widow of Cornelius Vanderbilt Whitney, married John

Hendrickson, thirty-two. He is a former state tennis champion, a former aide to Alaska's ex-governor Walter J. Hickel, and head of the company that manages Whitney's estimated $100 million fortune.

It was reported that a prenuptial agreement was signed at Hendrickson's insistence. "If something happens, I don't want her to be able to take my tennis rackets."

⅋

Who Gets the Booby Prize?

In 1999 Fox chairman and Dodgers owner Rupert Murdoch married Wendi Deng, thirty-two, two weeks after completing his divorce from Anna Murdoch. Comedy writer Jerry Perisho joked: "They would have married a week earlier, but there was trouble with the prenuptial agreement. In the event of a divorce, neither of them wanted possession of the Dodgers."

⅋

If Only They'd Had Pre-Nuptial Agreements

Adam might've eaten ribs without pain,
No Bobbitt cut-off date for Wayne.

Henry the Eighth might be less an oppressor,
Anne Boleyn could be headed for her hairdresser.

If only they'd had PNAs . . .

And was it Ms. Franklin's premarital right
When she told her Benjy to go fly a kite?

Could the Kramdens have honeyed on the moon,
Roseanne and Tom still be singing in tune?

If only they'd had PNAs . . .

Even now Tarzan would be swinging with Jane,
Clark Kent could bare his assets to Lois Lane.

Fred and Ginger could still be cutting rugs,
Romeo and Juliet might not have done drugs.

If only they'd had PNAs . . .

For Noah, custody of only one of each species,
Mao and the missus could still be sharing lichees.

When Tommy met Sally in ol' Virginny,
They could've been happy as Mickey and Minnie.

If only they'd had PNAs . . .

When they named the GW Bridge for our dollar man,
They wouldn't have reduced Martha to the lower span.

Hillary's health plan wouldn't have taken such a
trimmin'
And she could've sued Bill for his impeachable taste in
women.

If only they'd had PNAs . . .

They'd all have improved their lives 'neath the covers
If they'd had the good sense to read *Prenups for
Lovers.*

—Duke of Razumny

"See, it's right here in the prenup. If you walk out,
I get two weeks' sex severance."

POETIC JUSTICE

Pennsylvania Appellate Court judge J. Michael Eakin
was moved to poetry in rendering his decision to uphold
a prenuptial agreement in June 1999. He rhythmically
rejected the appeal of the husband, Conrad Busch, who
was barred from obtaining spousal support from his
wife upon termination of their marriage. While not exactly a Shakespearean sonnet, it does add some sorely
needed humor to legal casebooks:

The opinion, consisting of twenty-seven quatrains
of rhyming couplets, begins:

> Conrad Busch filed a timely appeal,
> trying to avoid a premarital deal

which says appellee need not pay him support;
he brings his case, properly, before this Court.

The judge used meter to cite the basic rule of law:

A prenup's a contract, and the parties are bound
to honor its terms if disclosure is found,
to include fair recital of what each one's got,
before it's put into the marital pot.

He lyrically resolved whether disclosure was proper:

The issue is fairness; were things fully disclosed?
Clearly her assets were completely exposed,
so enforcing the contract we cannot prohibit
for mere want of a staple attaching an exhibit.

Inspired by the romantic origins of the marriage,
Judge Eakin intoned:

They wanted to marry, their lives to enhance,
not for the dollars—it was for romance.
When they said "I do," had their wedding day kiss,
It was not about money—only marital bliss.

Judge Eakin finished with a flourish:

But a deal is a deal, if fairly undertaken,
and we find disclosure was fair and unshaken,
Appellant may shun that made once upon a time,
but his appeal must fail, lacking reason (if not
rhyme).

THE KING AND HIS SEVENTH QUEEN

Eternal nuptial optimist Larry King, the preeminent talk show host, reportedly did not require his seventh bride, Shawn Southwick, to sign a prenuptial agreement. But should we be taking marital advice from someone who's been married seven times?

PRENUPS: I LOVE YOU

There is a vintage Woody Allen joke about his relationship with his first wife. They couldn't decide whether to take a vacation in Bermuda for a weekend or get a divorce. They opted for the divorce, using the reasoning that it was something they would always have.

To update the gag, you might choose between getting a prenup or going to Bermuda for a vacation. Not only will the prenup be cheaper, but also you and your sweetheart will increase your chances for marital bliss. The prenup is something you will always have—in happiness and good health.

P.S. I hope you get to Bermuda, too.

APPENDIX 1. MARITAL LAWS BY STATE

State	Community Property*	Equitable Distribution*	Dual Property **	Unitary Property**	Has the State Adopted the Act?[a]
Alabama		X	X		No
Alaska		X	X[1]		No
Arizona	X		X		Yes
Arkansas		X	X		Yes
California	X		X		Yes
Colorado		X	X		Yes[4]
Connecticut		X		X	Yes
Delaware		X	X		Yes
District of Columbia		X	X		Yes
Florida		X	X		No
Georgia		X	X		No
Hawaii		X		X	Yes
Idaho	X		X		Yes

State	Community Property*	Equitable Distribution*	Dual Property**	Unitary Property**	Has the State Adopted the Act?^
Illinois		X	X		Yes
Indiana		X		X	Yes
Iowa		X	X[1]		Yes
Kansas		X		X	Yes
Kentucky		X	X		No
Louisiana	X		X		No
Maine		X	X		Yes
Maryland		X	X		No
Massachusetts		X		X	No
Michigan		X		X	No
Minnesota		X	X[2]		Yes[4]
Mississippi		X	X		No
Missouri		X	X		No
Montana		X		X	Yes
Nebraska		X	X[3]		Yes

State	Community Property*	Equitable Distribution*	Dual Property**	Unitary Property**	Has the State Adopted the Act?
Nevada	X		X		Yes
New Hampshire		X		X	No
New Jersey		X	X		Yes
New Mexico	X		X		Yes
New York		X	X		No
North Carolina		X	X		Yes
North Dakota		X		X	Yes
Ohio		X	X³		No
Oklahoma		X	X		No
Oregon		X		X	Yes
Pennsylvania		X	X		No
Rhode Island		X	X		Yes
South Carolina		X	X		No
South Dakota		X		X	Yes
Tennessee		X	X		No

State	Community Property*	Equitable Distribution*	Dual Property**	Unitary Property**	Has the State Adopted the Act?ª
Texas	X		X		Yes
Utah		X		X	Yes
Vermont		X		X	No
Virginia		X	X		Yes
Washington	X			X	No
West Virginia		X	X		No
Wisconsin	X		X¹		No
Wyoming		X		X	No

*See discussion in chapter 10, question 5.

** See discussion in chapter 10, question 7.

1. Courts distinguish between marital and separate property, but may invade separate property if equity requires.

2. Up to one-half of a spouse's separate property may be considered.

3. Definition of separate property provided by courts, not statute.

4. Most states that have adopted the Uniform Premarital Agreement Act (the "Act") have done so with some modifications to the Act itself. Colorado has adopted the Colorado Marital Agreement Act, while Minnesota has adopted the Married Persons; Rights and Privileges, which are both similar to the Act.

NOTE: To prepare the above chart, it was necessary to make subjective judgments to fit states into classifications. In addition, classifications may change as statutory and case law change.

APPENDIX 2. COHABITATION LAWS BY STATE*

State	Courts Recognize Express Cohabitation Agreements	Courts Recognize Implied Cohabitation Agreements	Courts Have Indicated Willingness to Award Equitable Remedies	Courts Refuse to Recognize Any Cohabitation Agreements	State Law Prohibits Cohabitation	State Law Recognizes Common Law Marriage
Alabama						✓
Alaska	✓	✓	No			
Arizona	✓	✓	✓			
Arkansas						
California	✓	✓	✓			
Colorado						✓
Connecticut	✓	✓	✓			
Delaware						
District of Columbia						✓
Florida	✓	✓	✓		✓	
Georgia	No	No	No	✓	✓	

State	Courts Recognize Express Cohabitation Agreements	Courts Recognize Implied Cohabitation Agreements	Courts Have Indicated Willingness to Award Equitable Remedies	Courts Refuse to Recognize Any Cohabitation Agreements	State Law Prohibits Cohabitation	State Law Recognizes Common Law Marriage
Hawaii	✓	✓	✓			
Idaho					✓	
Illinois	No	No	No	✓	✓	
Indiana	✓	✓	✓			
Iowa	✓	✓	✓			✓
Kansas	✓	✓	✓			✓
Kentucky	✓					
Louisiana	No	No	No	✓		
Maine						
Maryland	✓	✓				
Massachusetts	✓				✓	
Michigan	✓				✓	

State	Courts Recognize Express Cohabitation Agreements	Courts Recognize Implied Cohabitation Agreements	Courts Have Indicated Willingness to Award Equitable Remedies	Courts Refuse to Recognize Any Cohabitation Agreements	State Law Prohibits Cohabitation	State Law Recognizes Common Law Marriage
Minnesota	✓	No	No			
Mississippi	✓	No	No		✓	
Missouri	✓	✓	✓			
Montana						✓
Nebraska	✓	✓				
Nevada	✓	✓	✓			
New Hampshire	✓					✓[1]
New Mexico	✓	No	No		✓	
New Jersey	✓	✓	✓			
New York	✓					
North Carolina	✓	✓	✓		✓	
North Dakota	✓				✓	

State	Courts Recognize Express Cohabitation Agreements	Courts Recognize Implied Cohabitation Agreements	Courts Have Indicated Willingness to Award Equitable Remedies	Courts Refuse to Recognize Any Cohabitation Agreements	State Law Prohibits Cohabitation	State Law Recognizes Common Law Marriage
Ohio	✓					
Oklahoma	✓					✓
Oregon	✓	✓	No			✓[2]
Pennsylvania	✓	✓	✓			✓
Rhode Island						✓
South Carolina						✓
South Dakota						
Tennessee						
Texas	✓	No				✓
Utah						✓
Vermont	✓	✓	✓			
Virginia					✓	

State	Courts Recognize Express Cohabitation Agreements	Courts Recognize Implied Cohabitation Agreements	Courts Have Indicated Willingness to Award Equitable Remedies	Courts Refuse to Recognize Any Cohabitation Agreements	State Law Prohibits Cohabitation	State Law Recognizes Common Law Marriage
Washington	✓	✓	✓			
West Virginia	✓	✓	✓		✓	
Wisconsin	✓	✓	✓			
Wyoming	✓	✓				

*See chapter 17.

1. Only at death and if cohabitation is more than three years.

2. Only at death and if cohabitation is more than ten years.

NOTE: Courts in Florida, Hawaii, Indiana, Kansas, and New Jersey have not awarded property distribution based on the three theories for recovery identified above, express contracts, implied contracts, and equitable grounds, but have implied that different circumstances might warrant recovery under multiple theories.

NOTE: Some states that only allow recovery for express agreement, under limited circumstances, will allow recovery for business or financial agreements giving rise to implied contracts or partnerships.

NOTE: *Marvin* applies to homosexual and heterosexual couples with equal force in California. Some states that recognize express and implied contracts, as well as equitable remedies, do so only for opposite-sex relationships.

NOTE: Blank boxes in the first three columns signify that the law in each such state has not been clearly articulated.

NOTE: To prepare the above chart, it was necessary to make subjective judgments to fit states into classifications. In addition, classifications may change as statutory and case law change.

ACKNOWLEDGMENTS

To begin at the beginning: My sincere thanks go to Francis J. Greenburger, who directed my idea for a pro-prenup book for the public to his literary agency, Sanford J. Greenburger Associates, Inc.

I would like to express my great appreciation to Heide Lange, my super agent, who solicitously shepherded my book and me through the publishing process. She provided invaluable advice.

To Bruce Tracy, editorial director at Villard Books, Oona Schmid, assistant editor, and Katie Zug, editorial assistant: Thank you so much for your energetic commitment to this project as well as your top-notch editing skills. It was a joy to work with you, publicists Carri Brown, Brian McLendon, and Jynne Dilling Martin; production editors Nancy Inglis and Beth Pearson; designer Meryl Sussman Levavi; and the other members of your team.

My deepest gratitude goes to all my partners at

RubinBaum LLP, where I have had the good fortune to practice law for over twenty years. I thank all of you for your support of this project and patience in its execution. In particular, I would like to thank Ronald Greenberg, chairperson of our firm, for encouraging my efforts and providing wise counsel. To Allan M. Rosenbloom: Thanks for your help and for being a mentor and friend. To Denise M. Tormey: Thanks for your ongoing support and unique spirit. Special thanks to Brit L. Geiger, Paul V. LiCalsi, Martin P. Michael, Jane G. Stevens, and Michael J. Weinberger for providing your expertise. Certain of my other partners must be mentioned for a range of contributions: Thomas G. Barrett, Michael J. Emont, Paul A. Gajer, Martin R. Gold, Alvin J. Goldman, Raymond J. Heslin, Edward Klimerman, Christine Lepera, Matthew L. Lifflander, David A. Mandel, Stephen A. Marshall, Ivan W. Moskowitz, Marina Rabinovich, and Stephen L. Solomon.

Also at RubinBaum LLP, thank you to Julienne Amoroso, my dedicated secretary, who embraced every aspect of this project; Tania P. Danielson, our diligent librarian; Karen Kasny, assistant librarian; Keith Sharack, MIS director; Ellen Cook, word processing manager; Lisa Gardner, Website designer; Stella Orso, office manager; and lawyers Andrew Haskell, especially for his work on the charts in this book, Janet Harvilchuck, Anita Pomeranz, and Carol E. Wolk, as well as summer interns Deborah Allton, Elizabeth Lucas, Leslie Pappas, Elizabeth Shor, Carrie Teicher, and Eric Williams, and international "observer," French and Spanish lawyer Helena Bescos.

To all my clients: Thank you for inspiring me to write this book and providing some of the raw material on which it is based.

A special thank-you to Lorna Greenberg, writer and editor, who offered her keen insights on many aspects of this project—from proposal to manuscript.

I am grateful to my friend Ken Regan, photographer to the stars.

Many professionals in the mental health, spiritual, and financial fields participated in this project and are referred to in this book. They gave generously of their time, reflection, and expertise and provided much more than could possibly be quoted in a book of this size and scope. I am greatly in their debt. In particular, I would like to thank Dr. Ruth K. Westheimer ("Dr. Ruth") for sharing her perspectives on psychology as well as on writing books and also for her encouragement. Thank you to Dr. Samuel Abrams and Patricia Slatt, C.S.W., for their early and continuing professional assistance on this project. For their inspiration and input, I offer a special thanks to Rabbi Allan Schranz, Msgr. Edward Scharfenberger, and Al-Haaj Ghazi Y. Khankan.

Thank you so much to the following leading legal experts on prenuptial agreements for contributing your experience and wisdom: George S. Stern, Stern & Edlin, Atlanta, president of the American Academy of Matrimonial Lawyers; Gordon H. Marsh, Marsh & Valentine LLP, New York, chairperson of the Matrimonial Committee of the Association of the Bar of the City of New York; Jacalyn F. Barnett, New York; Larry A. Ginsberg, Harris-Ginsberg LLP, Los Angeles; and George A. Rustay, Dow Cogburn & Friedman, Houston.

To Philip Schwartz, Schwartz and Ellis, Ltd., Arlington, Virginia, president of the International Academy of Matrimonial Lawyers: Thank you for your assistance and for introducing me to an international community of matrimonial lawyers. The following lawyers enlightened me about prenups in their countries: Douglas Alexiou (England), Alain Cornec (France), Karen Kear-Jodoin (Canada), Ian Campbell Kennedy (Australia), Annelise Lemche (Denmark), Werner U. Martens (Germany), Frederic Renstrom (Sweden), Rolf P. Steinegger (Switzerland), and Carlos Zepeda (Chile).

Thank you to Barbara Abrams, chairwoman of my feminist reading group, and the members who shared their important perspectives on prenups: Phyllis Chalfin, Themis Dimon, Alisa Kieffer, Barbara Leiterman, and Sandra Van de Walle, Esq.

Many friends, colleagues, and experts provided assistance in various aspects of this book, and I thank them: Dr. Nathaniel Branden, Elissa Buie, C.F.P., Dominique Devriendt, Professor Robert Dingwall, Ellice Fatoullah, Esq., Dr. Nina Fieldsteel, John Flaxman, Steve Gelman, Ian Jackman, Hon. Gabriel Krausman, Eric Lasher, Maureen Lasher, Mel Powell, Kenneth Resen, Robert Rothenberg, Franziska Ruf, Dr. Clifford Sager, Alan Schnurman, Esq., Judy Stein, Richard W. Stevens, and Professor Hugh Wilson.

For a lifetime of togetherness and solid support, as well as concrete contributions to this book, I send my love and gratitude to my very dear siblings Lisa and Daniel P. Dubin, my sister-in-law and brother; my brother Dr. Gerald H. Dubin; Heather and Craig McDonald, my sister and brother-in-law; and my nieces and nephews: Allison Dubin and Christopher Tracy, Mindy Dubin, and Clifford, Jason, and Douglas McDonald. In addition, I want to acknowledge the entire Krumholz clan—my husband's warm and wonderful extended family (too numerous to individually mention) for their love and assistance. In particular, thanks to cousins Naomi Rivlin and Dr. Ellen Mandel for their inventiveness and special skills, and to Enid Glabman, my sister-in-law.

Many thanks to my precious daughter, Susan D. Schnier, who even managed to send me a Valentine's Day card containing a pre-Valentine agreement while I was writing this book ("Whereas, Be Mine!"). Susan shares my passion for writing and often exhorted: "Mom, it's all in your head. Just get it down." She also offered her usual critical and original thinking on the manuscript. Thanks to Susan's friends, in particular Hilary Kopple, Julia Marx, and Rachel Moss, for their help.

My mother and father, Dorothy and Milton Dubin, have been the ultimate inspiration in my life. I thank them for being married for over sixty years, always being there for me, and loving me much too much to possibly be deserved.

I conclude with a person whom it is impossible to thank enough: Bud Rosenthal, the mid-husband on the birth of this book, my live-in editor, and my partner in prenups and everything else.

INDEX

ABOUT THE AUTHOR

Arlene G. Dubin is a partner in RubinBaum LLP, a prominent New York City law firm, where she specializes in matrimonial law as well as employee benefits and executive compensation. Ms. Dubin has practiced law for over twenty years. She graduated cum laude from the College of Arts and Sciences at Cornell University and Brooklyn Law School, where she was editor in chief of the *Brooklyn Law Review.*

Ms. Dubin also holds a master's degree in journalism from the Columbia Graduate School of Journalism and worked as a journalist prior to becoming an attorney. She and her husband live in New York City and are happily married—with a prenup, of course.

Ms. Dubin can be reached at www.prenupbook.com.